LITTLE BOOK OF
THE LONDON
UNDERGROUND

Robin Bextor

LITTLE BOOK OF
THE LONDON UNDERGROUND

First published in the UK in 2013

© Demand Media Limited 2013

www.demand-media.co.uk

Printed and bound in China

ISBN 978-1-909217-37-9

Contents

The Tubeway Army of one Billion

If any institution could more readily come to stand for modern London than the Tube than I have yet to think of it. Practical, egalitarian, efficient, popular, logical, organised and yet infuriating, maddening, and confusing it stands for everything modern life does in this great World capital. For most of my life I have taken the Tube for granted, a huge resource that links me to my work, my friends, my entertainment and to every facet of life in this City.

The Underground is dependable, ever present-it's that gentle giant that rumbles in the distance, those familiar red circles on the street, and yet it wasn't always like that. But then London wasn't always like it is today.

Nowadays the tube carries over a billion people every year. It is the string that pulls together the leafy suburbs to the wheels of finance and commerce. Oxford Street is linked to Bank and to Epping or Ealing with one easy connection. The hip streets of Camden are but a stone's throw to the Heath of Hampstead, the fashionistas of Sloane Square just a few stops from the obscurity of Osterley. The Tube map is how we picture our great City, and where once upon time the River was the dominant mode of transport now the heir to the throne gets his free Oyster card and even Jeremy Clarkson concedes that the fastest way from West to East London is via the underground. For one hundred and fifty years the London

Underground has carried Londoners from all over the world around the capital, the first in the world, the biggest and of course the best.

For anyone visiting London a trip on the tube tells you everything you need to learn about being a Londoner. Connect from Heathrow to Piccadilly and you will see how we dress, how Londoners, from bonus chasing bankers to arty students at St Martins, travel to their work, what we read on our tablets, or on our laps, what we listen to, what fantastic diversity there is and what fashions are on their way up and down. You can read poetry on the walls, hear licensed buskers, get free papers, and just be in that throng of people that is London. It is also an equal opportunity travel system.

I remember a few years ago watching a film about the Rolling Stones and Mick

ABOVE Congestion on the London Underground. We're all familiar with the term 'Mind the gap' but it's more of a case of 'Fill the gap' during rush hour

Jagger was talking quietly to his London neighbour The Who's Pete Townshend. He was clearly incredulous of Pete's assertion that he used the tube to travel up to the West End from Richmond most weeks, he couldn't believe he went on his own without security and wondered in what class he traveled. Pete couldn't believe the street fighting man's lack of general knowledge.

Of course there are no classes now on the Underground, they went years ago, it is the same seats for all, and everyone gets on and off at the same platforms, travels at the same speed, minds the same gap and experiences the same delays. It is a truly democratic institution. Ken Livingstone brought thousands back onto the tube and they have stayed, it just makes sense. When I worked at Thames TV back in the 80's I can clearly remember getting on the train home from Warren Street and finding myself sat next to the young (ish) GLC leader- at least he practiced what he preached!

A few years ago I moved away from London to Sussex. Instantly I realised how much I missed the tube. That connection with people and places was somewhere else. That ease of transport, and a " one ticket goes everywhere" mentality had gone. But last summer with the Olympics in the East End we went back and found that it was not only still there, but better than ever - wifi connected, full of people from all over the world and in the throes of a stylish modernization.

That's the thing about the Tube, 150 years old this year and it is truly a story of 150 years of evolution and development. And it hasn't ended here either, just like London constantly reinvents itself and moves on then the Tube continues to grow, to link more places, to drop one or two of the less popular stations, and to become the system that defines its age. The numbers keep growing; it is a long way from hitting the buffers.

It's the place the American Werewolf romped unfettered, it's the station at midnight that Paul Weller immortalized, we are all in the army Gary Numan enlisted, and we think of Gerry Raferty as we rattle through Baker Street. When you hear that rumble it really is London calling.

Our story tries to reflect something of the character of the Tube and therefore of London itself, and it starts when there was no tube at all, in fact London didn't even know it needed one....but it really did and how!

Robin Bextor
2013

ABOVE 55 Broadway, St James's Park station and the HQ of London Transport aka Frank Pick's castle

Chapter 1

Before the Tube

The birth of the London Underground of course was in 1863, 150 years ago, but the origins of the underground go back way before that.

In fact the reasons for having an underground at all stem from the unrivalled and rapid growth of Victorian London as the capital of the global Empire, the first industrial power base and the epicenter of the modern world. Just look at how the population boomed.

When James I came to the throne in 1603 London's population stood at just a little under 150,000 inhabitants, or about the same number that attend the home games of Fulham, Chelsea, Spurs and Arsenal over a weekend (if

they all played at home on the same Saturday-which they don't, but you get the point).

And of those 150,000 many of them lived in country manor houses and estates, the economy was still largely agrarian and the focus of life was towards the countryside. At the Restoration of Charles II in 1660, it was calculated by John Gaunt a Fellow of the Royal Society, that there were about 120,000 families within the walls of London. "The trade and very City of London," he says, "removes westward, and the walled City is but one-fifth of the whole pile." Before the Restoration, says Sir William Petty, the people of Paris were more than those of London and Dublin

put together, "whereas now (1687) the people of London are more than those of Paris and Rome, or of Paris and Rouen." Petty's figures differ occasionally; but the result of his inquiries seems to have been, that in 1682 there were about 670,000 people in London, and the Population Returns of 1801 (113 years afterwards) put the figure at only 864,845. So slow, albeit steady, growth.

But in the 19th Century all those piffling increases changed. Thanks to the introduction of the census, and the thorough organisation that Victorian society brought to bear, we can see that London went from under a million at the start of the century to a massive 6.7 million by the end of it.

London swelled and rapidly assumed

the role of the world's largest city. It just went ballistic. During this period, the city became a global political, financial, and trading capital. In this position, it was largely unrivalled so the growth was completely unfettered. International trade, the dominance of the oceans, the massive engineering and industrial growth and innovation (as showcased in the brilliant Olympic opening ceremony at London 2012) headed by genius skills from men such as Brunel, Bazalgette, and Stephenstone meant that the whole nature of life changed. And it changed rapidly.

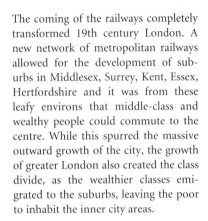

BELOW A view of New Cross on the London and Croydon Railway, 1839. The station is to the left of the road bridge. The London and Greenwich Railway on viaducts is visible in the background

The coming of the railways completely transformed 19th century London. A new network of metropolitan railways allowed for the development of suburbs in Middlesex, Surrey, Kent, Essex, Hertfordshire and it was from these leafy environs that middle-class and wealthy people could commute to the centre. While this spurred the massive outward growth of the city, the growth of greater London also created the class divide, as the wealthier classes emigrated to the suburbs, leaving the poor to inhabit the inner city areas.

The poor therefore provided the workforce at the bottom of the ladder, while the middle rungs were filled by those who needed to get to work to fill in the ledgers, count the imports, insure the boats, staff the growing civil service and so on. In other words society changed from agricultural to industrial and London was at the forefront. Business demanded that technology somehow came to the rescue, and of course it did.

During the beginning of the 19th Century London was awash with horse manure. Hundreds of thousands of horses pulled carriages, dragged drays,

tugged barges, took up precious Mews space, clogged the streets and generally made life dirty and inconsistent. By the 1830's that was about to all change.

In 1836 the first railway to be built in London was constructed, a line from London Bridge to Greenwich. This was soon followed by the opening of a series of great railway stations, which linked London to every corner of Britain. These included Euston station (1837), Paddington (1838), Fenchurch Street station (1841, Waterloo (1848) King's Cross (1850), and St Pancras Station (1863).

ABOVE An early print of Euston station showing the wrought iron roof of 1837. Note the open carriages

BELOW Queen
Victoria opens the
Great Exhibition in
the Crystal Palace in
Hyde Park, London
in 1851

The trains not only filled a need, and were a benefit to society; there was more than philanthropy to their development. It was a way to get rich, and the London underground would offer the same inducement.

In 1851 the Great Exhibition, pretty much devised and produced by the Prince Regent, held at the Crystal Palace in Hyde Park, showed the world just how far London had come. There were the exhibits that proclaimed we had the best engineers, the greatest tradesmen, the cleverest craftsmen and of course everyone wanted to come and see. The result was a new phenomena-the day-tripper. Never before had anyone

dreamed of popping up to the capital to take in a show. And what Prince Albert did next with the profits from the Great Exhibition cemented this social trend.

With quite brilliant foresight he created a new area of London nicknamed Albertropolis, which was packed with great things to see on your day off-the Victoria and Albert museum, the Albert Hall, the Science Museum, the Natural History Museum all within a short hop of each other. No wonder there is a memorial to him and he brought us the Christmas Tree-what a Royal!

Meanwhile the urbanised area continued to grow rapidly, spreading into the North and into Islington, to the West and Paddington, Belgravia, Chelsea, Kensington, areas like Holborn and Finchley, Shoreditch, Southwark and beyond. Add to that the construction of some landmark buildings, the creation of Trafalgar Square, Big Ben, the Houses of Parliament, Tower Bridge and you get the picture. This was a new London with sights and attractions that needed visiting, with work that needed to be clocked in at, with stations that needed connecting, with families out

in the suburbs not all living in the same village and they needed to be able to see each other...something had to help people get about the place, keep those wheels turning, there was money to be made and in looking for the answer everyone agreed on one thing: it wasn't the horse anymore.

ABOVE Drawing of a dial for the Clock Tower of the Palace of Westminster, also known as Big Ben by Sir Charles Barry, 1838. Note the clock face is coloured blue in the drawing, rather than black as in the completed structure

Chapter 2

So What Next?

In the 21st century there is an integrated Transport for London system that includes the underground system and also London buses, light Docklands Railway, trams and the over ground rail system. In the early 19th Century everything was a bit more hit and miss, in fact the development was strictly on an entrepreneurial basis.

With almost 500,000 horses regularly on the streets of London hauling everything from private carriages and cabs to delivery vans, and motorized transport some way in the future it was inevitable that the first solutions to London's problems should be horse-drawn as something was needed right away to keep the city on the move,

GET ON THE OMNIBUS

First into the ring was George Shillibeer and his Omnibus. Now obviously the Bus was a great idea, much copied and certain to succeed but unfortunately it was not a success for George. He copied the basic idea from France-where the name Omnibus came from – it was actually in Nantes in 1823 where one of the first bus stops was outside a hatter's shop. The hat shop had a big sign up "Omnes Omnibus" omnes meaning "all" and omnibus meaning "for all" in Latin- so everything for everyone. The title caught on as a name for the transport system.

Shillibeer was born on 22 October 1797; he was a talented engineer/carpenter

who worked for a coach company. In the 1820s he was offered work in Paris where he was commissioned to build some unusually large horse-drawn coaches of "novel design". The aim was to design a coach capable of transporting a whole group of people, perhaps two dozen, at a time.

Shillibeer's design worked, and was very stable. It was introduced into the streets of Paris in 1827. Shortly afterwards, he was commissioned to build another by a girls' school in Newington capable of carrying 25 or so pupils. This was the first school bus.

SO WHAT NEXT?

While he was working in Paris George concluded that a similar system could work in London, but with multiple stops and the public paying for the pleasure of using it.

So Shillibeer set about creating an omnibus service opening on 4 July 1829 along the route between Paddington and Bank a key route into the City along New Road. Four services were provided in each direction daily. This service was described in the first advertisements as being "upon the Parisian mode" and that "a person of great respectability attended his vehicle as Conductor". An

BELOW George Shillibeer's first omnibus

account of the new service was given in the Morning Post of 7 July 1829:

Saturday the new vehicle, called the Omnibus, commenced running from Paddington to the City, and excited considerable notice, both from the novel form of the carriage, and the elegance with which it is fitted out. It is capable of accommodating 16 or 18 persons, all inside, and we apprehend it would be almost impossible to make it overturn, owing to the great width of the carriage. It was drawn by three beautiful bays abreast, after the French fashion. The Omnibus is a handsome machine, in the shape of a van. The width the horses occupy will render the vehicle rather inconvenient to be turned or driven through some of the streets of London.

But despite the reassurances offered to the gentry (who were not used to sharing transport) the service did not take off. The fares were far too high and also the buses did not get close enough to where the workplaces were. Within a year poor George had to leave London in a hurry to escape his creditors-he fled to France

where his former boss and the innovator of the Parisian busses had already committed suicide. It seems so obvious that bus travel would work, but you had to get it right.

Fortunately for George he created a horse drawn funeral carriage that restored his finances, and there is even a pub commemorating him in Caledonian Road. He died in Brighton in 1866.

HAIL A CAB

Of course the method of transport that had been favoured up till then in the City is still around today-notably the Hackney Cab based on Captain Bailey's Hackney Coaches from the 17th century. Bailey had started a service at the Maypole Inn at St Mary in the Strand and in 1654 Cromwell authorised the Fellowship of Hackney Coachmen. By 1662 there were 300 licenses issued for hackneys at a fee of £5. They really had the monopoly on wheeled public transport for centuries and of course today there are about 16,000 licensed taxis in London. The word cab incidentally came about in 1823 when a two seater was introduced by a chap called David

Davies and he called it a cabriolet from the French, and it soon shortened to cab.

THE CRYSTAL WAY

By the 1850's a Parliamentary select committee was set up to look into ways of improving Metropolitan transport. After the Great Exhibition of 1851 the buzzword was clearly "Crystal" and in 1855 William Moseley came up with a

ABOVE Hackney Coach Sign in Colinton. A self-explanatory sign set into a wall in Woodhall Road. The inscription reads, "5 miles from the G.P.O. Edinburgh. Erected to regulate the post horse duties payable by hackney coach 1824"

SO WHAT NEXT?

BELOW The front entrance of the Crystal Palace, Hyde Park, London that housed the Great Exhibition of 1851

Crystal Way to transport passengers in some style.

This was one of several schemes for enclosing the route of transport just like the Crystal Palace, enclosing the route in glass. Moseley, an architect, thought that a railway just below street level could run from St Paul's Cathedral to Oxford Circus, with a branch off to Piccadilly Circus.

The plan was to cover the track with a wrought iron grid, free of traffic, which could be a pedestrianised area and they would pay a penny to walk the length of the way and watch the trains below. The footway would then be enclosed within a crystal canopy, so the whole thing would be like an enormous conservatory full of shops, flats, and hotels.

The trains would be pneumatic railways, driven by atmospheric pressure so there would be no pollution. The cost was to be about £2 million, but there was a decidedly big downside in the plan; there was no connection to the main line stations, which was really the main point of the exercise. The scheme sunk.

PAXTON'S GREAT VICTORIAN WAY

There were at least two other Crystal solutions to the transport problem but it was the creator of the Crystal Palace himself- Sir Charles Paxton - who came up with the most ambitious scheme: he proposed a 12 mile long railway system that linked the mainline stations, crossing the Thames three times while so doing.

Just like the other schemes it would be encased in a crystal arcade with shops, houses and all the paraphernalia of a modern mall, but without the young folk in hoodies.

In this way he argued the stench of the river would be avoided and a more benign climate created akin to living abroad for those fortunate enough to live in the arcade, but with no need to speak a strange language or eat croissants.

There was one thing working against the plan though and that was the massive cost as it was estimated at £34 million, an absolute fortune in 1855 not simply the fee for an average striker…and that was that for the Great Victorian Way.

THE ARCADE RAILWAY

But the sheltered idea was not altogether stymied, and it was a radical thinker, typical of the Victorian age, called Charles Pearson who created a working scheme that really got the whole underground system moving.

BELOW Caricature published in Punch on 21 July 1855 (page 27) in response to Michael Faraday's letter "Observations on the Filth of the Thames", published on 7 July in The Times and commenting on the deplorable state of the River Thames

CHARLES PEARSON

Charles Pearson (4 October 1793 – 14 September 1862) can legitimately claim to be the father of the Underground system. He was not an engineer though or financier but more of a social reformer. He had successfully persuaded the City's authorities to admit Jews to the freedom of the City of London, and also had some objectionable anti Catholic inscriptions removed from The Mon-ument. He was a reforming campaigner, and – briefly –MP for Lambeth. He campaigned against corruption in jury selection, for penal reform, for the abolition of capital punishment, and for universal suffrage, votes for everyone. But most of all he was a crusader for equality and protecting the increasing poor-especially those living in dire conditions in the capital. He was ahead of his time and altruistic to the core.

Recognising the increasing congestion in the City and its rapidly growing suburbs Pearson published a pamphlet in 1845 calling for the construction of an underground railway through the Fleet valley to Farringdon. The proposed railway would be an atmospheric system-and by that I don't mean it had background music and moody lighting- the trains were pushed through tunnels by compressed air. Although the proposal was ridiculed and came to nothing Pearson continued to lobby for a variety of railway schemes throughout the 1840s and 1850s. He did not give up because he saw there was a purpose and a benefit to improving the City's transport.

Pearson's aim in promoting the plan was to improve the living conditions of City workers by enabling them to commute into London on cheap trains from new residential developments of good quality, cheap homes built outside the capital.

In 1854, Pearson tried again with a plan for a railway connecting the London Termini and presented as evidence the first ever survey of traffic coming into London. It demonstrated the high level of congestion caused by the huge number of carts, cabs and omnibuses filling the roads. Pearson's commentary on this was that:

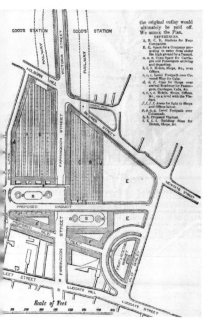

The overcrowding of the city is caused, first by the natural increase in the population and area of the surrounding district; secondly, by the influx of provincial passengers by the great railways North of London, and the obstruction experienced in the streets by omnibuses and cabs coming from their distant stations, to bring the provincial travellers to and from the heart of the city. I point next to the vast increase of what I may term the migratory population, the population of the city who now oscillate between the country and the city, who leave the City of London every afternoon and return every morning.

The commission of 1854 did not accept everything he said, or adopt all the proposals but the key decision was reached: it recommended that a railway was to be built linking the stations, and allowing commuters to travel between Paddington and the City, on August 7 of that year a bill was passed suggesting just that.

Now Pearson's scheme had a real chance and London was about to change forever.

LEFT Proposal by Charles Pearson (1793-1862) for a central railway terminus for London. The illustration shows the planned layout of the station centred on Farringdon Street between Fleet Street and Holborn Hill, with capacity for four railway companies 'A', 'B', 'C' and 'D' and expansion space for one more, 'E'. The railway lines arrive from the north. Despite much lobbying from Pearson, the station was never constructed

Chapter 3

The Metropolitan Line

Charles Pearson was neither a significant shareholder nor a director of the new company that became known as the Metropolitan but he continued to promote the project over the next few years and use his influence to help the company raise the £1 million needed for the construction of the line. Throughout he really did appear to be the misanthropist the age demanded rather than seeking personal profit, and he saw the building of the line as a genuine case of improving social well being -improving communications but at the same time doing something to remedy some of the awful housing conditions in the area.

He issued a pamphlet, a twenty minutes letter to the citizens of London, in favour of the Metropolitan Railway and City Station, encouraging investment and he even persuaded the City of London to invest on the basis that the railway would alleviate the City's congestion problems. Once the railway was in operation, the City sold its shares at a profit. By 1860, the funds had been collected and the final route decided. Work on the railway started taking less than three years to excavate through some of the worst slums of Victorian London and under some of the busiest streets.

Pearson's proposal consisted of a railway running from Bishop's Road Farringdon to King's Cross in an arcade open to the sky above but below street

level with room on either side for street traffic to pass.

The City corporation had been planning to clear slums from the area North of Ludgate Circus anyway and Pearson calculated that about 50,000 people – who were living in dreadful conditions-could be moved to "artisan" cottages in the land to the North of Kings Cross. Each would have a bit of garden. He proposed that none of the new trains should be allowed to charge more than a penny per mile and that it would be a great step forward both in living conditions and progress for the capital.

So Pearson's utopian scheme combined with some hardheaded investment realism resulted in a well-budgeted and organised approach that ticked the boxes for the politicians.

Meanwhile, however, another proposal was being formed: termed the Bayswater, Paddington & Holborn Bridge. This would run west from King's Cross to a terminus under Sussex Gardens, near the present Lancaster Gate station. The line would run under what was then called the New Road and is now Euston Road (this had, incidentally, also formed part of the first horse-drawn bus service in London - Shillibeer's line from Paddington to the Bank - back in 1829). The Paddington Vestry objected to the Sussex Gardens terminus, and so the BPHB cut back their proposed route to terminate in the area of the present Edgware Road station. The company was renamed the North Metropolitan Railway, and received its Act of Parliament in 1853.

Rather than building the line as authorized, the North Metropolitan arranged a merger with the City Terminus Co., allowing an end-to-end route to be contemplated. The NMR owners were mostly interested in local traffic, and they dropped the proposals for extra tracks and a major terminus. This also helped reduce opposition to the plan, for some people wanted the main-line railways to advance no further south into the city (and, indeed, none ever did). Instead, a terminus under the General Post Office at St-Martin's-le-Grand was proposed; this would allow the convenient carriage of mail.

Meanwhile at the western end the line would be extended along Praed Street to the front of Paddington station, and there would be a link to the main line as well; in return, the GWR agreed to invest in the railway, which would be built with mixed gauge track (even though the 1853 Act explicitly forbade the provision of standard-gauge rails between the main line and Praed Street Junction).

The resulting merged company was renamed the Metropolitan Railway and got its new Act in 1854. Both endpoints were changed yet again before the line was actually constructed: in the east it was cut short to Farringdon, while in

ABOVE Electric
locomotive and train,
Metropolitan Railway
(CJ Allen, Steel
Highway, 1928)

the west the Paddington station terminus was moved from the front to the north side of the GWR station, where it did not need to be underground.

Furthermore, by diverting the main route on to what would have been the link to the GWR, it was possible to eliminate about 500m of tunnel to the original station.

The line was immediately popular - within a few days of opening additional trains had to be scheduled running non-stop from Paddington to Farringdon to handle the extra demand.

Powers were also obtained during construction for an easterly extension to Moorgate; as soon as the line had opened, money was easily raised and the work was swiftly done.

The money was one concern at the time; another was how the trains would be powered. Steam locomotives were the only practical possibility, but main-line experience showed how slowly smoke and steam would dissipate from tunnels. Furthermore, unlike normal railways, the Metropolitan would have a frequent service with many closely spaced stations in the tunnels.

Metropolitan Railway fireless locomotive "Fowler's Ghost". This is the only known photograph of this locomotive. It is standing near Edgware Road station on the Metropolitan Railway in about 1865

tunnel sections, allowing the hot bricks to heat water into steam for propulsion. However, the prototype was such a failure, hardly able to move itself, that it gained the nickname "Fowler's Ghost" named after Sir John Fowler, chief engineer of the line.

Instead, the actual service was operated from the opening day right up to electrification with "condensing" locomotives, where the exhaust steam was diverted into water tanks. As the steam would heat the tank water to boiling, it had to be drained and replaced with cold water at the termini; this became impractical on completion of the Circle in 1884, and thereafter the drivers would sometimes have to release steam into the tunnels to keep the train from stalling.

The first proposal was for fireless steam locomotives, whose boiler would be filled with sufficient pressurized steam - fed from a fixed installation - at each end of the journey. But these had not yet been successfully developed and what was actually built was a locomotive with a mass of brick inserted around the firebox. The fire would burn intensely in the open-air sections of the line, then be damped down for the

In addition to the link with the GWR, there were three junction curves linking the Metropolitan to the GNR at King's Cross (two facing east - one from each side of the GNR line - and one facing west). During construction a further link was authorized: the LCDR built a branch from Herne Hill that extended over the river via Blackfriars to meet the Metropolitan at Farringdon. Later a chord was added from this line facing towards Moorgate.

BELOW Metropolitan Line Heraldry

RIGHT Railway Lines
near Farringdon Station
Picture taken from
Clerkenwell Road.
Farringdon Station
can be seen about 200
metres away. Note
the different types
of railway track -- to
the left, the London
Underground ones with
a live rail, to the right,
the Capital Connect
(once known as
Thameslink) lines with
the overhead power
supply. At street level,
Turnmill Street is to the
left and on the right is
the rear view of offices
on Farringdon Road

The opening year - 1863 - was not a smooth one. Apart from a tremendous incursion of the River Fleet-perhaps reminding the builders one last time that nature was a formidable opponent-came some man made wrangles.

Originally the Metropolitan did not own its own trains, but ran a service with broad-gauge GWR rolling stock; no services were run from other railways, and the King's Cross links were unused (the west curve was probably never used, in fact; the track was lifted in 1865 and for many years the tunnel was filled with spoil). But when it was decided to add services from the GNR, the GWR realized that the eastern end of the line would be at capacity and unable to accept the new services they were planning, resulting in a dispute over who would operate how many of the trains. The GWR set a short deadline after which it would withdraw the use of its stock. Instead of capitulating, the Metropolitan put into place a stock-building programme, and in the meantime borrowed replacements from the GNR and LNWR, enabling it to take over operations in August 1863 without a gap.

Incidentally, this required the GNR to hurriedly convert some engines to condense their exhaust steam (through a flexible pipe into the tender). Despite 6 derailments on the first day because the standard-gauge rail had not been aligned properly, the GNR stock worked successfully until the Metropolitan could introduce its own and it was returned to its owners the following year.

THE WIDENED LINES

The traffic on the eastern part of the route soon became heavy enough that the Metropolitan built a second pair of tracks from King's Cross to Moorgate. They were opened in 1868 and are called the Widened Lines or City Widened Lines - the term refers specifically to the newer tracks; they cross under the Metropolitan just west of Farringdon station, being on the south side from there to Moorgate. The Widened Lines took the services using the connections from the GNR and LCDR, as well as a new one from the Midland Railway's extension to St. Pancras (in fact, this link opened over two months before St. Pancras itself). A section of tunnel about 360m long was dug under the forecourt at St. Pancras, and could have been used to extend them further west (probably to allow a connection to the LNWR at Euston), but no track was laid in it.

As the Widened Lines' original purpose was through running from the main line railways, it is fitting that they are now part of the NR Thameslink route; they are no longer connected to LU at any point. Indeed, the only time that Underground trains used them in service was from 1926 to 1935.

A new link was installed from a new junction called Chalton Street Junction, west of King's Cross, connecting the original eastbound track to the eastbound Widened Line in the unused tunnel under St. Pancras (extending it about 210m). This allowed eastbound trains terminating at Moorgate to pass under the main westbound track rather than crossing it on the level.

LONDON'S OWN EIFFEL TOWER

Not everything the Metropolitan line touched turned to gold though. It is not widely known but London could have had a tower to rival the attraction of the Eiffel Tower in Paris.

Following the success of the French monument in 1889 the Metropolitan sponsored a similar but larger (353m or 1159') Wembley Tower, and in antici-

RIGHT Metro-Land booklet were published annually from 1915-32 by London's Metropolitan Railway. This is the cover of the 1921 edition, which promoted housing in the area served by the railway

pation of the large crowds it would draw opened a new station at Wembley Park to serve it.

A competition for the design was held, an architectural firm won the bid and a structure together with plans for restaurants, observation decks and even a Turkish bath in the sky were drawn up. But all was not so good. When the egocentric chairman of the company Sir Edward Watkins left in 1901 so did the impetus for his project...and the funding.

Only about the first 60m (200') of the tower was built as problems with the foundations meant it was starting to topple; the venture was a financial disaster and the structure was removed after being dynamited in 1907, allowing the land to be used for building.

Part of the area was reused in the 1920s for the Empire Exhibition and for Wembley Stadium. To serve these a separate Exhibition station was opened in 1923 on the east side just south of Wembley Park station, with non-stop trains to Baker Street; this remained until 1937, when it was replaced by an additional platform at the main station. The remains of the tower were found when the new Wembley Stadium was built in 2000-a few tangled lumps of metal where the foundations had been laid.

METROLAND

For much of its independent life, the Metropolitan was known for encouraging commuter traffic and new development on "green-field" sites; this policy was supported by a unique legal position that allowed the company to own property for building rather than being required to sell off the land not needed for railway use. Both the Watford and the Uxbridge branches - and the Stanmore branch now part of the Jubilee Line - were built for this reason, and the new developments that followed became known as "Metroland" a term first appearing in publicity material in May 1915 and more recently popularised by the late Poet Laureate Sir John Betjeman and of course Julian Barnes in his 1980 novel.

Mock Tudor-bethan houses were built, lifestyles advertised and suburbs around

Pinner and Wembley created. The term "Metroland" (note the hyphen) was first used by the Met's marketing department when the Guide to the Extension Line became the Metro-land guide, priced at 1d. This promoted the land owned by the railway out near the Chilterns as a rural nirvana for the commuter. It was described as a place to walk, think, observe nature and raise a family. The dream promoted was of a modern home in beautiful countryside with a fast railway service to central London.

It was also the only Underground line to run Pullman coaches (two luxury coaches with catering facilities, owned by the Pullman Car Company) in its trains. In 1931 it even fitted chocolate vending machines in some trains.

METRO-LAND

PRICE TWO-PENCE

BUSY BUSY

Whatever your opinion of Metro-land and the strange almost Orwellian concept of such managed living, the scope and spread of the Met was amazing. Chesham, Watford, Aylesbury, Wotton, Ruislip are all a long way from Baker Street and with the linking systems to Oxford and beyond it was a startlingly ambitious undertaking.

Present-day Underground services operate only as far as Amersham, while main-line trains from Marylebone run as far as Aylesbury Vale Parkway. Beyond there, the line remains as a goods route (and distances along it are still officially measured from Baker Street the HQ of the Met,) though north of Quainton Road it follows the route of the GCR to its intersection with the LNWR line from Cambridge to Oxford, where a connecting curve was built during World War II.

Main lines now operate to places like Great Missenden, and the other stations that are no longer part of the Underground they form part of that long list of former Underground stations-or Ghost Stations.

The two Metropolitan routes have vanished. Operation of the Wotton Tramway ceased in 1935, after which its owners sold the track for scrap and let the route merge back into the countryside. The sparse passenger service to Verney Junction via Winslow Road was withdrawn the following year in order to make an annual saving of £42. Goods services along the route lasted until 1947, after which it was mothballed for 11 years before the track was eventually lifted.

THE IMPACT OF THE MET

When it opened, the Metropolitan Railway had a significant and detrimental impact on street traffic which was not an entirely bad thing, unless you happened to run the cabs and omnibuses. On the other hand though such was the population explosion and the influx of rural workers to the town that these quickly recovered to near their former levels, despite the Metropolitan Railway carrying over nine million passengers in its first year of operation. I wonder what their projections had been, but nine million travelers exceeded all expectations.

ABOVE Construction of the first underground line in continental Europe, Budapest, 1896

The Metropolitan Railway and the network of underground lines that grew from it was the first in the world and the idea was not adopted elsewhere until 1896 when the Metro in Budapest and the Subway in Glasgow were both opened.

The timing was everything, without Pearson's promotion of a covered railway when he did it is possible that transport developments at the end of the 19th century, such as electric trams and vehicles powered by internal combustion engines, might have meant that the underground solution just never happened.

The expansion of the capital that the underground network and its suburban surface extensions enabled was considerable and incredibly rapid and helped the population of what is now Greater London to increase from 3,094,391 in 1861 to 6,226,494 in 1901. It was the largest City in the World.

Pearson died of dropsy on 14 September 1862 at his home at West Hill, Wandsworth and sadly did not live to see the opening of the Metropolitan. Naturally he had refused the offer of a reward from the grateful railway company but, shortly after the line's opening, his widow was granted an annuity of £250 per year that she accepted.

Pearson was buried at West Norwood Cemetery on 23 September 1862. I think he would have been proud of what the Underground has become, and now stands for. An equal opportunity transport company-once on board everyone is equal, the traveller can come from any background at all, but when in the carriage everyone is on the same footing, the companies have all become centrally operated by TFL under the auspices of a democratically elected mayor and the slums that dogged Victorian London have been replaced by mile upon mile of Metroland. All with their own gardens.

But contemporaneous records of the time have differing opinions about the coming of the Underground.

In the hand-book of London one commentator wrote:

BELOW A painting showing an intersection of the street with the Millenium Underground Rail (Metro line 1) beneath street level, Budapest, Hungary, 1896

UNDER LONDON TOWN

Most Londoners will remember that for the last two years the New Road has been blocked at various portions by gigantic hoards, at which, during day and night, steam engines were at work aiding the "navvies" in pulling up to the surface huge loads of gravel or of London clay. The public understood that these places were the shafts, sunk for the purpose of proceeding with a subterranean railway, which, having for its purpose the connection of the various huge lines running to the north, south, east, and west of England, would greatly facilitate the transmission of passengers through London, and relieve the streets of the enormous traffic. As the undertaking was one of great difficulty and cost, many prophets started with the positive assurance that it would be a failure; that it would never be commenced, or if commenced, never finished; that London would be undermined, blown up, or collapse on each side of the tunneling; and that these and half a dozen other evil presages would turn out true. It is with some pleasure, therefore, that, in duty to the public and the contractors, Messrs. Jay, and Smith and Knight, we have

to record the complete success of the work, so far as engineering goes, and to assure our readers that this most gigantic engineering work has been quietly and successfully carried on in London, in spite of immense difficulties, of shifting grounds, swelling clay, falling houses, bursting drains, and continued incursions of the Fleet Ditch—a small and extremely unpleasant London river of historical and poetical celebrity, the course of which has more than once been turned, and which is now carried over the railway.

The carriages are wide, high, and commodious, and lighted on each side by the compressed gas, so that one can very well read a newspaper by the light. The ventilation in the tunnel is very complete, and there is not the slightest smell, pleasant or unpleasant; indeed, the atmosphere, from the constant current of air, seems better than the ordinary atmosphere of the city. On the Saturday afternoon named, the eager shareholders and public flocked to the Victoria terminus, and after some little delay mounted the carriages, first class, second class, and trucks that had been prepared for them.

In about 700 yards, all tunnel, passing

under the old part of Clerkenwell and Bagnigge Wells, the graveyard of the paupers and their work-house, passing huge black boxes full of bones, which were being care- fully and decently removed to some suburban cemetery, we reached Frederick Street, where there is an open cut-ting, and thence to the first station at King's Cross. Much gratified surprise was expressed at the height, width, and convenience of the carriages, much at the pleasant atmosphere of the railway, and when we reached Gower Street station, much more at the pretty and even airy aspect of everything around us.

Although we were upwards of forty feet below the earth's surface, we found that it was as light as day daylight in fact being shed down upon us by ingen-ious contrivances in the forecourts of the houses and the street pavements.

Skylights are constructed horizontally from sidings of thick glass on a level with the pavement, and beneath these sidings a handsome cutting lined with white tiles admits, and at the same time reflects and multiplies the light ; and to the vaulted station itself huge oval eyelet holes, lined also with Minton's tiles, admit both light and air. The effect is very soft, cool, and even rural. Descending thither from a broiling day in the hot streets will be a pleasant change enough, whilst in winter the change will be varied by the passengers being protected from the cold winter blasts. The Portland Road station differs from that of Gower Street by being lighted by two large glass domes on a level with the street, and a flat skylight. Baker Street station is a reproduction of that of Gower Street, elegant, and economical; a sufficient regard being had to simple ornament and durability. Edgware Road station, near Praed Street, is lighted horizontally, as the railway then comes upon the open, many houses having been taken down for the purpose. After a safe journey, in which there was certainly something novel, curious, and encouraging, passing in and out

the deep shades thrown by the side lights in the tunnels, under the roar of a million passers-by, under gas-pipes and drains, houses and streets, without much noise, save of the cheering of the passengers, without inconvenience, smoke, smell, or dust, with no oscillation, and with perfect safety, we again returned, riding in the open trucks, admiring the stanch brick work of the tunnels, the fine spring of the arches, and the clean way in which all the work was done, and emerged from the regions of the earth pleased with the journey and satisfied of the future success of the undertaking, which will surely pay the shareholders, as it has been constructed, it is said, under the estimate of £1,500,000.

The Metropolitan Railway will not only be an eminently successful undertaking, but also a great national benefit.

The Times newspaper focused more on the class divide (or lack of it) and the comfort of the carriages:

Between one and two o'clock thousands of anxious travellers by the new route were collected outside the Victoria-street terminus, and when the outer doors were opened, which was only at intervals, the

LEFT "The Metropolitan Underground Railway" poster, 27 December 1862 rush was tremendous, and on reaching the ticket office the difficulty of exchanging cash for a ticket was an equally difficult task. The platform gained, the next grand struggle was for a seat in the incoming and presently outgoing train. Classification was altogether ignored, the holders of No.1 being obliged to be compelled to go in No.3 or not at all, and vice versa. Hundreds on each occasion, however, had to be left behind, to take their chance of the next train in rotation. Of the general comfort in travelling on the line there can be no doubt, and the novel introduction of gas into the carriages is calculated to dispel any unpleasant feelings which passengers, especially ladies, might entertain against riding for so long a distance through a tunnel. Yesterday, throughout every journey, the gas burnt brightly, and in some instances was turned on so strong in the first-class carriages, in each of which there were two burners, that when the carriages were stationary, newspapers might be read with facility; but, in motion, the draft through the apertures of the lamps, created so much flickering as to render such a feat exceedingly difficult. The second-class carriages are very nicely fitted with leathered seats, and are very commodi-

ous, and the compartments and arms in the first-class render overcrowding impossible. There is one point to which attention was attracted as being adverse to the general expectation, and that was that it was understood that there was to be no steam or smoke from the engines used in working this tunnel railway. All we can say is, that on one of the journeys between Portland-road and Baker-street, not only were the passengers enveloped in steam, but it is extremely doubtful if they were not subjected to the unpleasantness of smoke also. This may have arisen from the circumstance before alluded to, that in consequence of the extreme pressure upon their resources, the workers of the metropolitan line were compelled to avail themselves of locomotive as well as rolling stock of the Great Western, and that it is only a temporary inconvenience. Up to six o'clock the computation was that somewhere about 25,000 persons had been carried over the line, and it is gratifying to remark that, notwithstanding the eagerness of the public to get into the carriages, even when the trains were in motion, no single accident, of any kind, was reported.

The Times, January 11th, 1863

TODAY

Now The Metropolitan line connects Aldgate in the City of London, the capital's financial heart, with Amersham and Chesham in Buckinghamshire, with branches to Watford and Uxbridge. Coloured corporate magenta on the tube map, the line serves 34 stations in 41.4 miles (66.7 km). The track and stations between Aldgate and Baker Street are shared with the Circle and Hammersmith & City lines, between Rayners Lane and Uxbridge with the Piccadilly line, and between Harrow-on-the-Hill and Amersham with Chiltern Railways trains.

In 1863 the Metropolitan Railway began the world's first underground railway service between Paddington and Farringdon Street with wooden carriages and steam locomotives, but the most important route became the line north into the Middlesex countryside, where it stimulated the development of new suburbs. Harrow was reached in 1880, and the line eventually extended as far as Verney Junction in Buckinghamshire, more than 50 miles (80 km) from Baker Street and the centre of London. The steam trains ran until 1961 when the line was electrified to Amersham and London Transport services to Aylesbury withdrawn. The Hammersmith & City line was shown on the tube map as part of the Metropolitan line until 1990 when it appeared as a separate line.

The track is underground only in the central London section between Aldgate and Finchley Road and of the 34 stations on the line, just nine are below ground. Almost 67 million passenger journeys were made in 2011/12.

BELOW Today millions of passengers use Oystercards on the London Underground as well as many of the other forms of public transport in London

Chapter 4

Architecture

The architecture of the Underground system is iconic, and yet far from monolithic. The different companies involved in the early construction and the use of different architects has allowed for some marvelously quirky constructions and also some interesting construction glitches such as Leinster Gardens in Queensway that defy rationale explanation. There the observer can see the mock frontage of two large buildings that disguise a huge absence behind, just a void where a massive canyon was created by the digging for the Metropolitan line.

Both 23 and 24 Leinster Gardens are less than six feet thick have painted windows and no letterboxes, in fact the whole façade is just a bit of stage setting although you have to look closely to be able to tell.

This is a posh area, make no mistake, so to save money the properties on either side of the digging and construction work were not purchased, the trains simply rattle between the houses barely under the ground at all. (see pictures) and the front of the road does not reveal a thing.

But above surface and at the stations there has always been a connection between the lines and either their surroundings or an element of the arts and modernity.

When it came to design the boss of the

Underground during its' most influential era in the 1920's and 30's Frank Pick selected work by, amongst others, artists Walter Gropius and Edward McKnight Kauffer. Both made poster design a serious art form, bringing ideas from Germany inspired by the Bauhaus that pushed the avant-garde into the mainstream in the UK.

The same principle applied to the architecture on the tube during Pick's reign. He worked hand in hand with an uncompromising and inspired architect, Charles Holden. Holden is probably, with Leslie Green, the most prominent station architect. He based Arnos Grove on Stockholm Public Library and the Moscow Metro inspired Gants Hill. Holden was a minimalist at heart and believed that artifice and cornicing, twiddly bits and ornaments should all be banished-clean lines and form everything. He came from a penniless background, worked as a railway clerk before his brother helped him become an architect. His stations are often simple, geometric and listed. The booking hall at Piccadilly is a classic, he added the international clocks as a symbol of modernity, and as with other stations he wanted to use modern materials, make everything "fit for purpose", cut out extraneous details and exert the influence of the Bauhaus.

It was Holden who built the HQ above St James Station, which was the tallest building in London when it opened in 1929. He championed the work of modern sculptors with work from Jacob Epstein, Eric Gill and Henry Moore.

The other great architect of the system was Leslie Green. All 46 stations designed by Leslie Green have distinctive tile patterns to help regular customers recognise them. Green's stations – such as Covent Garden – were all steel-clad to allow premises to be built on top of them.

More recently Sir Norman Foster designed Canary Wharf station, which opened in 1999 as part of the Jubilee line extension. and if anything carries on the tradition of Pick and Holden then it is the modernism of the Jubilee.

Some of the most interesting stations from a design point of view are:

TOTTENHAM COURT ROAD

Tottenham Court Road has to be one of the jazziest stations on the system. There is a huge mosaic by pop artist Eduardo Paolozzi. Installed in the 80s the frieze is clearly inspired by life above

ground nearby, these feature everything from the rainbow saxophones of Soho's jazz clubs to masks from the British Museum.

BAKER STREET

Baker Street with its timber-paneled ticket hall and soaring brick barrel vault, lit by grand globe lanterns, is a station that instantly transports you back to another era – chiefly that of Sherlock Holmes, whose pipe-smoking silhouette adorns tile after tile Baker Street as the kingpin station of the Met can lay claim to be London's oldest tube station, built in 1863 for the Metropolitan Railway, the world's first line. There's still a sign above the ticket office saying: "Luncheon and Tearoom."

SOUTHGATE

Southgate is just a mad station from the outside. It looks more like a space craft than a station with its circular design, it has to be most futuristic of the stations designed by Charles Holden with the spacey looks and art deco adornments designed during a creative spurt in the 1920s and 30s. Its slender white roof

juts out like the brim of a hat over a cast-iron frieze; above this float a lantern and coil, seemingly about to shoot a bolt of lightning down to the tube with other Electrical symbols about the place. It also has a really moody escalator with great lighting.

BELSIZE PARK

Belsize Park is one of the 50 Edwardian stations designed in just four years by the astonishingly prolific Leslie Green and it has all of the best Green trademarks: semi-circular windows and oxblood red tiles – all developed as a low-cost way of building stations for just nine shillings (45p) per foot. There is also a hidden air-raid shelter, designed for 8,000 people –now leased to a data storage company.

WESTMINSTER

There are few more thrilling experiences to be had on the tube than descending into the Blade Runner-esque platforms of Westminster Station, below the gothic hi-tech of Portcullis House. Designed by Michael Hopkins in 1999 and short listed for the Stirling prize, this dramatic concrete well is woven with stacked banks of escalators that hang from a dynamic network of flying concrete beams and steel tubes. Chains and darkened shadows shroud hidden shelving and moody corners, allied to a modernistic industrial atmosphere.

BOSTON MANOR

Between 1932 and 1934 the station was rebuilt to replace the 1883 original building. The new station was designed by Stanley Heaps in the modern European style used elsewhere on the Piccadilly line by Charles Holden. The design uses brick, reinforced concrete and glass. Occupying a narrow site because of the approach to the adjoining depot, the station was built out over the tracks. The distinctive tower feature, with an illuminated leading edge and roundel rises high above the low structure and helps identify the station from a distance. It was strongly influenced by contemporary Dutch and German architecture and was intended to create a landmark building amid an area of low-rise suburban housing.

RUSSELL SQUARE STATION

Russell Square is a typical Leslie Green designed station. Best features are the tiles, which are outstanding, and there are excellent surface level examples of the half circular large "window" design Green favoured. It feels sturdy, substantial and welcoming. There is also a poignant tiled monument to the victims of the 7/7 attacks.

ABOVE The half circular large "window" design at Russell Square station

ABOVE The ox-blood red glazed terracotta blocks at Mornington Crescent station

MORNINGTON CRESCENT

Mornington Crescent is another Green classic, opened on 22 June 1907 and now fully listed. On 23 October 1992 the station was closed for the renovation of the lifts, but although the intention was to re-open within 12 months it wasn't until six years later that the cast of I'm 'Sorry I Haven't a Clue' were able to cut the ribbon. The lovely Samantha was taken up with something else that morning. There is a bar over the road named after the former host of the programme Humphrey Lyttelton . Incidentally Belle and Sebastian have a track named after the station on their Life Pursuit Album.

The ground level station buildings like the one at Mornington Crescent were designed to a uniform Arts and Crafts style, which was adapted to suit the individual station location. They were constructed as two-storey buildings with a structural steel frame — then a new form of construction recently imported from the USA. The steel frames provided the large internal spaces needed for ticket halls and lift shafts. They were clad in non-load bearing ox-blood red glazed terracotta blocks, with the ground floor divided into wide bays by columns and featuring large semi-circular windows at first floor level and a heavy cornice above.

The station buildings were constructed with flat roofs with the deliberate aim of encouraging commercial office development above, another benefit of the load-bearing structural steel frame. At platform level, the stations were provided with a standardised tiling design incorporating the station name, but with quickly identified individual colour schemes and geometric tile patterns formed in repeating panels along the platform length.

But Green did not enjoy the fruits of his considerable labours. The deadline for having all of the stations in his remit up and running was tight, they were to open in 1906 and 1907 and the pressure of producing designs and supervising the works to so many stations in such a short period of time, placed a strain on Green's health. He was elected a Fellow of the RIBA in 1907, but contracted TB and died in the summer of the following year at the age of 33.

Many of Green's station buildings survive, although internal modifications have seen most of his ticket hall designs altered to suit later developments. At platform levels a number of the original tiling schemes survive today or have, as at Lambeth North and Marylebone, been reproduced in recent years to the original pattern. Three of the surviving stations namely Holloway Road, Mornington Crescent and Gloucester Road are listed buildings.

In 1903 Heaps (the man who designed Boston Manor) had became assistant to Leslie Green, following the early death of Green in 1908 Heaps became the UERL's architect and produced designs for a number of new stations right into the 1920's.

Heaps' first independent station designs were for the four new stations on the Bakerloo line extension which opened in 1913 and 1915. Although not the first London Underground stations to be provided with escalators those four stations of Paddington, Warwick Avenue, Maida Vale and Kilburn Park were the very first stations to be designed specifically for their use. In other words they did not use lifts at all, as had the original Bakerloo line stations opened less than ten years earlier.

All of Green's designs had that characteristic second floor to house the lift drives, but by using escalators, Heaps' stations did not require a second floor to accommodate plant and they were designed as more modest single-storey buildings featuring tall windows each with a broad, tiled transom separating the curved top section to reflect Green's design.

So add the names of Heaps and Green to that of Holden and the Underground has been blessed with three architects and countless designers who really took their considerable task to heart in providing a large element of style to our daily journeys.

Chapter 5

The District Line

The Metropolitan was not the only company that wanted expansion of the London lines. With typical Victorian vigor and the entrepreneurial spirit of the age many proposals were put before a Select committee of the House of Lords, which had been set up in 1863, and the following year a joint committee set up by both houses tried to untangle the often conflicting and varied schemes.

It was clear that all the London mainline termini needed linking, and both ends of the Metropolitan could be extended to bring in more of the capital. The goal was to try and create a circle line but it was some time before this state of nirvana was reached. But it was

with this goal that the District Line started. To begin with the District was an offshoot both corporately and physically of the Metropolitan Railway. It was called The Metropolitan District Railway and was essentially a Blackfriars extension line running beneath the Victoria Embankment which had been created by the brilliant engineer Sir Joseph Bazalgette when he had rationalized the sewer system of the capital. The filthy foreshore of the Thames was reclaimed and a Southern cross route across London created.

So at the start the District was essentially a shuttle service, using Metropolitan rolling stock. It opened on Christmas Eve 1868 linking Westminster and

Blackfriars and then proceeded to head further South and West to the salubrious and seemingly profitable areas of Kensington via Victoria although to begin with no direct link with the main line station was created (that came with a subway in 1878.)

By 1869 the MDR reached Earl's Court (the first to have escalators some years later), and over the next few years through linkages with overground lines the network spread outwards and westwards. On 5 May 1878 the Midland Railway began running a circuitous ser-

THE DISTRICT LINE

ABOVE Interior of a District Line train

However the Super Outer Circle idea was not a success and was ended on 30 September 1880 but the District Line remained, with eastward expansion to Upminster and even at one time Southend although this was later seen as a step too far.

Even with all this expansion the finances were never far away from perilous though. The costs of creating the line were massive, the value of some of the housing stock that needed to be purchased before under digging was vast, the Westbourne River had to be capped and piped under ground near Sloane Square, and all of the £3 million initial investment was soon spent.

vice known as the Super Outer Circle from St Pancras to Earl's Court via Cricklewood and South Acton. It operated over a now disused connection between the NLR and the London and South Western Railway's branch to Richmond via the junction at Barnes. it combined forces with the south western railway to run out to Ealing and Wimbledon.

The split from the Metropolitan came after a series of particularly unpleasant and seemingly childish spats. Despite this both companies had their own rolling stock and the system continued to expand. It was James Staats Forbes who lead the District Line for almost 30 years from 1872 and who kept the business afloat and out of the hands of his bitter rival Sir Edward Watkin, the chairman of the Metropolitan Railway.

While Watkin was aggressive, hectoring and bullying then Forbes remained sanguine, charming and affable. Somehow the two larger than life characters co-existed but an even bigger character was on the horizon ready to stamp his authority on the whole system and the story of London's underground - one Charles Yerkes. Something had to be done to end the rather straggly and opportunist expansion and stabilize the service.

But more of him later.

Now the District has over 60 stations and approximately 450 miles of track, much of it not underground at all. In fact only 25 of its stations are below ground level. The District also has more bridges over the Thames than any other line with two…in fact no other line has any at all ! Some 18 trains an hour run between Earls Court and Tower Hill,

with 12 heading on out to Upminster in the East. In 2011 over 200 million passengers used the District Line and probably more than any other line it can claim to draw in passengers from right across the Capital's housing and geographic spectrum.

BELOW Two District Line trains, both composed of 'D 78' stock, await departure from Richmond on District Line services, 3 April 1985

Chapter 6

The Time Line

1863 The world's first underground train line, the Metropolitan Railway, opens from Paddington to Farringdon Street.

1868 What becomes the District line opens between Westminster and South Kensington on Christmas Eve.

1869 The East London Line opens between Wapping and New Cross.

1884 The Inner Circle (now Circle) line opens, connecting the Metropolitan and District lines.

1900 The Central line opens between Shepherd's Bush and Bank.

1905 The District and Circle lines switch from steam power to electricity.

1906 The Piccadilly line opens from Hammersmith to Finsbury Park and the

Bakerloo opens between Baker Street and Kennington Road.

1911 Earl's Court becomes the first station to install escalators.

1924 The Northern line opens, joining the City and South London Railway with the Charing Cross, Euston and Hampstead Railway.

1933 Draughtsman Harry Beck devises the first "diagrammatic" tube map, still used today.

1940 Tube platforms are used as air raid shelters throughout the Second World War.

1953 A collision in the tunnels outside Stratford station kills 12 passengers.

1968 The Victoria Line opens after 25 years of planning and construction.

1975 The worst crash in the history of the tube kills 43 people at Moorgate station.

1979 The Jubilee line opens, running between Charing Cross and Baker Street.

1987 A fire at King's Cross station kills 31 people.

2003 Oyster cards are introduced and busking is legalised in tube stations.

2005 The 7/7 terrorist attacks kill 39 passengers in tunnels near Liverpool Street, Edgware Road and King's Cross stations.

2007 The London Underground reaches a record one billion passengers in a single year.

2012 The London Olympics show the Underground dealing in style with record numbers.

ABOVE A 1992 stock tube train at the eastbound platform of Newbury Park tube station, sporting TfL's campaign 'Get Ahead of the Games' which helped provide information relating to transport during the Olympics

LEFT The title of this Chromolithograph is "Metropolitan Railway, Bellmouth Praed Street", and shows a GWR broad gauge train at Praed Street junction near Paddington station looking towards Edgware Road. The first services on the Metropolitan Railway 1863 were provided by the GWR

Chapter 7

The men on top of the Underground

CHARLES PEARSON is the founding father behind the Underground. He published a pamphlet in 1845 calling for the construction of an underground railway through the Fleet Valley to Farringdon.

The proposed railway would have been an atmospheric railway with trains pushed through tunnels by compressed air. Although the proposal was ridiculed and came to nothing Pearson continued to lobby for a variety of railway schemes throughout the 1840s and 1850s. He knew it was the way ahead. He was unwavering and through his pioneering blend of vision and philanthropy, he pushed through the approval of the first line.

THE MEN ON TOP OF THE UNDERGROUND

SIR EDWARD WATKIN (1819-1901) was responsible for the building of the Manchester Sheffield & Lincolnshire Railway's London extension during the 1890s, which was the last main line to be constructed into London. He was chairman of four rail companies and known as the second rail "king" after George Hudson. Contributed to the Canadian rail network and, in fact, to railways all over the world. Specialised in turning a profit from loss making situations, had a massive ego and unbelievable energy. Tried to build a London tower to rival the Eiffel, and also planned a cross channel tunnel.

JAMES STAATS FORBES (1823-1904) was born in Aberdeen, and with a streak of financial acumen that some would say was inherited turned struggling railway lines into profitable companies. He turned down the chance to work alongside Brunel on the Great Western Railway (and with it some footballer level wages) and instead rescued both a Dutch railway company, the London Chatham and Dover Railway and the District Line. He chaired the company from 1872 to 1901 and spent most of his time warding off his rival Sir Edward Watkins the boss of the Metropolitan and the South Eastern Railway.

LEFT Caricature of Sir EW Watkin MP, Vanity Fair, 6 November 1875

BELOW Caricature of James Staats Forbes, Vanity Fair, 22 February 1900

FAR LEFT Charles Pearson, circa 1855

THE MEN ON TOP OF THE UNDERGROUND

SIR JOHN FOWLER (1817-1898) was the chief engineer of the Metropolitan railway. You can see him in the photo taken on the opening day sitting alongside Gladstone. Born in Sheffield he was a child of the industrial revolution and worked as a civil engineer in the cutting edge railway industry. He designed both the locomotives and the permanent way for the Metropolitan line and became incredibly wealthy in so doing. He designed with Benjamin Baker the Forth Bridge, and later became chief advocate of the District line. His name was linked with the ill starred Fowler's Ghost loco but also helped design Victoria station and in building railways all over the world.

SIR JOSEPH BAZALGETTE (1819-1891) although not strictly a railway pioneer was instrumental to the infrastructure that allowed London to have an underground. He was chief engineer to the Metropolitan Board and as such designed the main sewers, which protected the capital's water supply and turned the Thames into a clean (ish) river. He also built the Victoria, Albert and Chelsea embankments replacing sewage-strewn foreshores with riverside land fit for development and rail lines. He constructed the Thames bridges at Putney, Hammersmith and Battersea.

THE MEN ON TOP OF THE UNDERGROUND

JAMES GREATHEAD (1844-1896) pioneering and hugely well paid engineer who helped with the Tower subway under the Thames, and became resident engineer on the Hammersmith extension railway and the Richmond extension of the District Line, a post he held for four years. Designed the engineering shield that allowed the tunnels to be dug but developed into a businessman behind the City and South London line amongst a number of ventures.

LEFT Caricature of Albert Grant MP, published in Vanity Fair, 21 February 1874

BELOW James Henry Greathead, circa 1890

ALBERT GRANT (1830-1899) was born in Dublin with a different name and a peddler for a father. He became an MP in 1865 but had to quit after allegations of bribery. He then spent £26,000 buying and refurbing Leicester Square and then donating it to London. He died in 1899 after a huge Bachelors Ball at an enormous house he built in Kensington-he died totally in debt and the staircase of the house was seized and sold to Madame Tussauds where it is today. Managed to derail early investment in the East London Line.

THE MEN ON TOP OF THE UNDERGROUND

CHARLES TYSON YERKES (1837-1905) was an American tycoon with experience of operating electric tramways in Chicago. But this is merely the outline-he could lay claim to being the most colourful character in the history of the Underground. He went to prison, loved art, women, money and combining any of the above whenever and as often as possible. He was also an expert in arranging the complex financial structures necessary to raise the capital the railway companies needed. His finances were always complex, and less stable than he portrayed. In 1900, he came to London and took over the District Line forming the Metropolitan District Electric Traction Company and raised some funds. He then took over the Brompton and Piccadilly lines with the sole aim of gaining a monopoly of the underground system. Within five years of coming to London he had electrified the Met and the District, built the lines that would become the Charing Cross branch of the Northern line and the central section of the Piccadilly, plus he acquired a tram company and fused them all into one-the forerunner of London Transport. He fought off JP Morgan and brought over American elevators, American escalators and did away with "Church" hour which was when the trains stopped running for a time on Sundays. He also ran the lines later and opened earlier, and had the same vision as Pearson that of clearing London of slums, setting the population out by 20 miles or so and then training them in to work. And don't forget a crater on the Moon is named after him and he built the Lots Road power station. He also died before he saw all of the schemes come to pass. His name rhymes with turkeys.

THE MEN ON TOP OF THE UNDERGROUND

SIR EDGAR SPEYER (1862-1932) was a New York banker out of Germany. He became chairman of the Underground Electric Railways Company of London from 1906 to 1915 ostensibly to keep an eye on what was happening to his banks' funds after Yerkes had spent them all, a period during which the company opened three underground railway lines, electrified a fourth and took over two more. He rescued the company from the financial machinations of Yerkes although he did steer a path that Yerkes would have approved of . He took British citizenship in 1892 and made substantial charitable contributions. During the war was accused of collaboration with the Germans and ended up in exile and finally died in Germany.

GEORGE GIBB (1850-1925) was manager of the North Eastern Railway when he was asked by Speyer to become manager of the cash strapped Underground Electric Railways of London. He introduced an analysis of traffic patterns, and had experience with electrification. Six days before Yerkes died he accepted the job, earning a massive £8k per year. He soon learned that losses were huge-the District was down £60k a year, so he slashed overheads, merged the management of the four different lines and brought in Frank Pick.

LEFT Portrait of Sir Edgar Speyer by Sir William Orpen, 1914, exhibited at the Royal Academy, London

BELOW Sir George Gibb, 1900–1910

BELOW Frank Pick, 27 January 1939

RIGHT Albert Stanley, 1st Baron Ashfield, chairman of the Underground Electric Railway, and his daughter Marion Stanley at the reopening of the City and South London Railway, 1 December 1924

FAR RIGHT Harry Beck, creator of the famous diagrammatic Underground map

FRANK PICK Managing Director of the Underground Group from 1928 and Chief Executive of the London Passenger Transport Board from its creation in 1933 until 1940. Pick can be portrayed as the real hero of the history of the Underground. He had a vision, and a style like Lord Reith at the BBC. A Quaker and a solicitor he joined North Eastern Railways before moving to the Underground group with George Gibb in 1905.He was in charge of marketing and publicity at first but later took over as vice chairman. He worked long hours, turned up unannounced at stations, sent letters in green ink displaying an unerring eye for detail, design, style and efficiency. Turned down state honours.

LORD ASHFIELD (1874-1948), born in Derby as Albert Stanley but grew up in the USA where at just 14 he worked for the Detroit Street Railway. He became manager of New Jersey tramways at 29 and on the insistence of shareholders who had invested in the London underground system was sent to the UK to keep an eye on George Gibb. He became general manager of the UERL in 1910 to 1933 and chairman of the London Passenger Transport Board from 1933 to 1947.

HARRY BECK, a London Underground employee who, in 1931 after being made redundant, devised the famous diagrammatic map.

also championed the cyclist in London, bus lanes, and launched the bid for the Olympics of 2012.

KEN LIVINGSTONE, Red Ken (born 1945) was a local politician who became the first Labour leader of the GLC in 1981. He made London Transport his priority. He introduced Fare's Fair, got the Tube working again after a dip in numbers and upgraded the whole transport system. He introduced the congestion charge and Oyster cards; he

Chapter 8

The Bakerloo Line

The route of the Bakerloo includes the oldest attempt at a tube railway, not just a cut and cover line. In 1865 the Waterloo & Whitehall Railway was given authority to construct a pneumatic railway (that is a line where the trains are pushed though a tunnel by air pressure) from Great Scotland Yard to Waterloo station. The single cast iron tube, 3.89 m (12'9") in diameter, would have crossed the river by being laid in a ditch dredged in the bed of the Thames. Though work did start, financial problems prevented additional capital being raised, and the work was abandoned in 1868, with the company being wound up in 1882. The trench excavated at the northern end is now the wine cellar of the National Liberal Club-so presumably had to be quite large.

In the same year an electric railway - the Charing Cross & Waterloo Electric Railway Company - was proposed to run from Trafalgar Square to Waterloo station. It would in the main have been a subsurface line and would have crossed under the Thames in twin cast-iron tubes. Again the idea failed to obtain the required funding and only about 20 metres of tunnel was built.

The real Bakerloo Line was created as the Baker Street & Waterloo Railway, intended to connect those two points via Charing Cross, a route that already had very heavy bus traffic. But as usual cash was in short supply. A mining

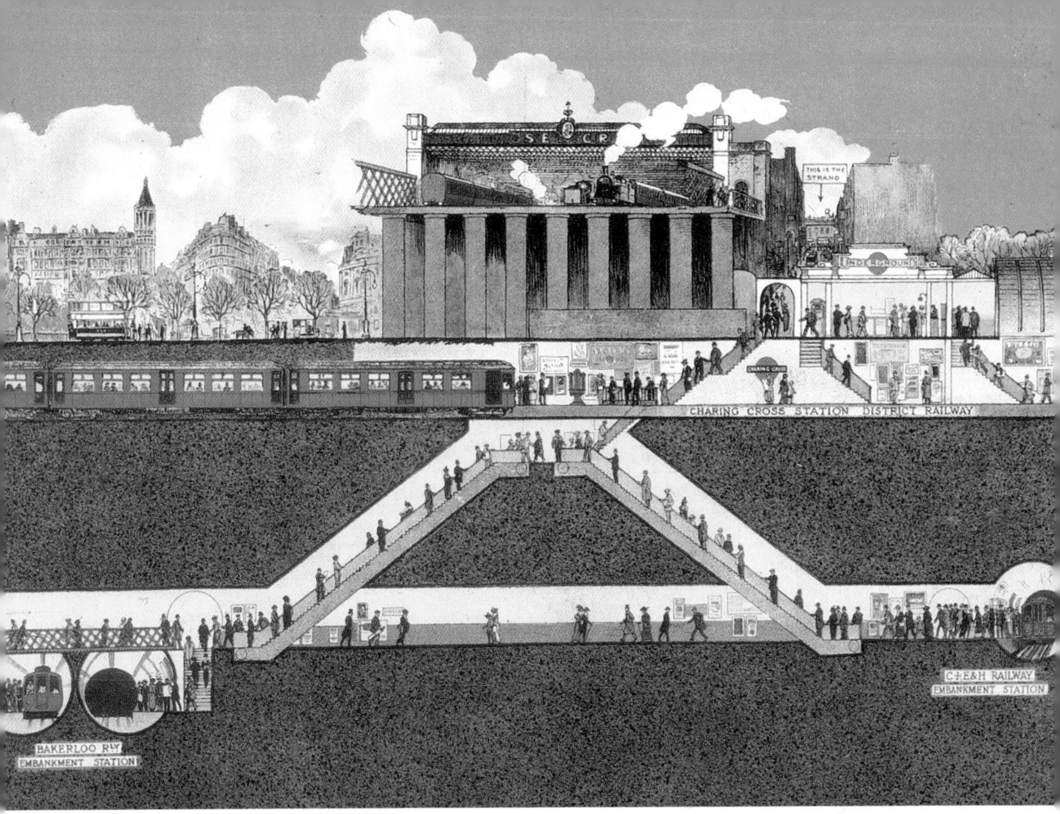
SE CR
THIS IS THE STRAND
UNDERGROUND
CHARING CROSS STATION DISTRICT RAILWAY
C+E&H RAILWAY
EMBANKMENT STATION
BAKERLOO RLY
EMBANKMENT STATION

engineer Whitaker Wright (1845-1904) stepped in when the scheme was on the point of floundering financially. In 1897 he managed to raise £700,000 from the City and despite opposition from rival lines (most notably the shy retiring Edward Watkins who complained that it was a little electric line blocking his magnificent scheme of a Manchester to Paris line) construction work started the following year.

And then it stopped, amidst financial chaos and Wright deciding to run off

ABOVE Section of poster "The New Charing Cross" from UERL advertising opening of Charing Cross, Euston and Hampstead Railway extension to Charing Cross Underground station, London, 1914

BAKER STREET & WATERLOO RAILWAY 1904

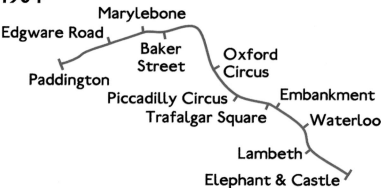

ABOVE Geographic Map of the Baker Street & Waterloo Railway, 1904

to France to avoid the creditors. They were persistent though, so Wright then fled to New York, but justice was not to be denied and he was hauled back to face charges of fraud. In front of the judge he eventually was found guilty of obtaining almost £5million through the use of fraudulent balance sheets and accounts whereupon he was sentenced to seven years in jail.

Wright left court a defeated man, gave his lawyer his gold watch, telling him "I will not need this where I am going" and proved the point by instantly drop-ping dead. He had taken a concealed cyanide capsule. A loaded revolver was also found on him.

So the plans for the Bakerloo were in disarray with at least three attempts to build a suitable line all floundering. At this point in its history the Bakerloo line came under the control of the same larger than life American as the District. Enter Charles Yerkes.

Yerkes had cut his teeth on the US rail system making money from the Chicago transport system. He arrived in London in 1901 and acquired the District Line and then the half built Bakerloo within a year. His ambition was to take over the whole system and was certain that electrification was the way forward. The huge Lots Road "Chelsea Monster" was the result of this thinking and eventually it supplied the whole of the underground.

Under Yerkes the construction of the line continued, a fresh rights issue of shares-based on largely over optimistic forecasts raised more money and despite Yerkes death in 1905 the line was completed and opened in March 1906.

The name Bakerloo came from the deceased London Evening News who hyphenated it, and despite opposition from the company as being too colloquial the name stuck and then became official. The year after it opened the line was extended to Edgware Road.

Yerkes' company the Underground Electric Railways of London (UERL) introduced a modernity and uniformity to the underground system. Staff wore uniforms; through the architecture of Leslie Green the stations had a utilitarian elegance. Square and windowed surface stations, with ticket halls, those distinctive blood red tiles, American elevators and escalators, and longer running times with high passenger numbers. Next line to fall in with Yerkes' scheme was the Northern but before that we need to recollect the Circle's origins.

BELOW Portrait of Charles Tyson Yerkes by Jan van Beers who arrived in London in 1901 and acquired the District Line

Chapter 9

The Circle Line

To discover the origins of the Circle line we have to step back a few years from Yerkes and his electrified lines. The Circle is not really a network or independent line at all in the true sense of the word but a collection of parts of other networks strung together and painted yellow to give the impression of being a fresh new line.

The early success of the Metropolitan Railway prompted a huge number of proposals for other railways. Parliamentary committees in 1863-4 evaluated them and decided that the best thing would be an "inner circuit" connecting both ends of the Metropolitan route (then Paddington and Farringdon) with the main-line railway stations on the north side of the Thames but serving the south (Victoria, Charing Cross, Blackfriars, and Cannon Street).

The idea was basically to close together the two lines of the District and the Metropolitan at Tower Hill and create the much-vaunted Circle. But the theory proved far easier than the practice. The Met and the District had a disparity in wealth and also in methodology. Right from the start the Metropolitan shareholders turned down the chance to merge companies-mainly because they did not want to take on the District's debt and that set the tone.

By October 1884 the Inner circle came

ABOVE Circle Line train leaving the platform at High Street Kensington

into being using both companies' trains, running on both companies' lines, which were already carrying other trains from the main services. So there was clutter. Add to that the terrible state of relations between the bosses of the two companies and you get the pic-ture...at the opening they were invited to share a carriage on the first journey. They did so but did not exchange a single word.

Metropolitan trains ran clockwise around the outer line, while the

WAIT HERE FOR
THIRD CLASS

WAIT HERE FOR
FIRST CLASS

ABOVE High
Street Kensington
Underground station
in 1892. Picture
shows signs showing
where the First and
Third class coaches
will arrive. Most First
class journeys on the
underground were
discontinued in 1940 as
part of the war effort

District's ran the other way on the inner. Tickets were stamped with an O or I (outer or inner) depending on which way you went, and of course this lead to passengers being directed to go the long way round because it benefited one company or the other. The wear and tear on the trains also was unbalanced because they were always going in

one direction, and when they did break down access was difficult to get them out of the way. So there were delays.

There was more: a dispute over the use of a siding at South Kensington came to a head when the District left its locomotives there and returned to find that the Metropolitan had taken them away. Next day the District left them there again but this time chained them to the rails. In response the Met sent three loco's to haul them away, and eventually a tug of war resulted with the rails being damaged and the train leaving the track.

So that early decision to reject the merger appeared short sighted. By rejecting the District's financial obligations, the Metropolitan acquired an enemy. For years thereafter, the story of the Circle line was the story of petty squabbles and strife. In fact the relationship only really became friendly after the completion of electrification in 1905 and the consequent improvement in the District's finances.

Since then the Circle Line has mostly operated unchanged. It gained its own identity in about 1949, although the name appears on a 1936 poster; until then the Inner Circle was just one of the services run by the Metropolitan and District Lines. In fact only the short section of the Circle from Aldgate to Minories junction (near Tower Hill) is exclusively Circle Line, everywhere else is Met, District or Hammersmith and City.

Now it carries about 70 million passengers a year, serving 27 stations over 14 miles of track, with a complete circuit taking almost exactly an hour to travel the whole circle.

BELOW The approach, High Street Kensington Station, 2010

Chapter 10

How on Earth was it All Built?

October 1859 and the first stretch of Underground London was undertaken. Just three years and three months later and the line was opened, an amazingly quick completion by modern standards, but those early tube lines were not "Tube" lines at all, and were barely underground.

The principle behind the construction was called "cut and cover" and basically consisted of laying the rails into what was in effect a trench or shallow grave. This was laid under the road-in this case the New Road running from Euston, in a brick cutting and then a roof was built over the tracks. So if you wish to be technical what they actually built was a bridge over the railway and put a road on it. But to all purposes this formed a tunnel for the train to run in.

Sometimes the crown of the tunnel-the highest point- would be less than a foot below the surface of the road. The cut and cover lines are the Metropolitan, the District, the Hammersmith and City and the Circle, which as we have seen, if you study the map looks more like an amalgam of several lines than a totally independent line in its own right.

Building under existing roads was both easier and cheaper, there was no need to purchase rows of houses for a start, but the rivers were the big enemies. The Fleet had to be piped and calmed, the Westbourne restrained and even to

this day over a million gallons of water are pumped from Victoria Station every day most from the Tyburn.

The majority of those early Metropolitan stations had domed glass roofs, allowing light to spill into the Dickensian depths. Many have now passed away to be replaced by more utilitarian structures but Notting Hill station still has a fine example on the District line platforms.

The trains themselves look very differ-

ent too, using wider gauge rails. The first photo of Gladstone on board one of the carriages sitting with his wife on board - is in an open wagon, everyone in hats of course. Later the Tube lines would have a narrower gauge, which explains why some cut and cover line drivers still refer to driving them as driving "Hornbys' that is model trains.

The Tube lines also had separate tubes for each direction whereas the cut and cover lines had both the "up" and

ABOVE View of a platform on the Baker Street and Waterloo Railway in its first week of opening, 17 March 1906

ABOVE The London Underground in 1890

passengers in the tunnels "to allow more air in", so they had to be rounded to prevent hitting the walls.

There were no waiting rooms, but there were plenty of signs showing the way for 3rd Class/2nd Class and 1st class passengers and licensed bars staffed by underpaid women who would work 11 hour shifts, for 10d a day. There were even subterranean sleeping rooms for the bar staff to doze in. As late as 1978 there was a bar on the platform of Liverpool Street and The Hole in the Wall at Sloane Square only closed in 1985-the same year smoking was banned on the Underground. It seems ridiculously recent.

"down" lines (ie the East and the West) laid side by side so you can see the trains going in the other direction, a treat missing from the Tube lines. So Tube lines were nearly always dug in tandem, one for each direction.

All the early Met stations have now been changed, the earliest survivor is Bayswater from 1868.The platforms had gas lights-yellowish domes burning with an ochre light. It must have been very atmospheric. The carriages were lit by gas too, and the doors, which opened outwards, would often be opened by

Trains traveled at about 20mph from the start, they ran at two minute intervals in the 'rush hour" and were shortened in length to allow less strain to be put on the engine which would mean less emissions. Of course the fumes were an issue, but by the time the government set up a serious enquiry in the 1890's the promise of electrification was on the horizon. But in fact steam loco's continued to run on the cut and cover lines until as late as the early 1970's!

DOWN DOWN DEEPER AND DOWN

The deep level tubes were a completely different phenomena to the cut and covers. To be built they required a way of tunneling deep into London's substrata, and also for the trains to be powered differently. Electricity did the second; the first was achieved through the invention of the tunneling shield. This allowed men to keep on digging while protected from the earth falling on them. It was invented by Brunel but not Isambard Kingdom but by Marc Isambard Brunel the genius's Dad.

Brunel snr. had devised the shield to dig under the Thames, he started his project in 1825 and 18 years later, after losing many men to floods, fire and illness the tunnel was complete. But it was not a business success; the investors had lost a lot of money and refused to cough up any more when it came to actually using the tunnel for anything. The scheme had been costly and the Thames-full of sewage as this was pre Bazalgette and his pipe system- was toxic. The investors just left the tunnel as a tourist attraction. In those days people were obviously

easier to entertain as you'd do well to get a queue of people to visit an empty tunnel nowadays and it was some time later that the next leap in technology allowed tunneling to progress. This was the Greathead shield, and in the 1890's it allowed greater flexibility for digging.

BELOW Memorial plaque for Marc Isambard Brunel and Isambard Kingdom Brunel seen in London's Transport Museum

RIGHT Plan of the City and South London Railway's station and depot at Stockwell as laid out in 1890. Subsequently, the station was rebuilt when the line was extended to Clapham. Image based on part of plan by James Henry Greathead's submitted to the Institution of Civil Engineers in 1890

Despite its' name-that came from the inventor James Henry Greathead- it was a smaller shield than Brunel's-weighing in at just two tons not the massive 120 tons of Marc's giant, Six men could dig at the earth face and an iron sleeve then was pushed forward, with liquid concrete pumped into the gaps. It was rather like a giant dustbin lid that the diggers could operate behind. It must have been a really arduous task and the work conditions were both laborious in the extreme and hazardous.

Anywhere from 40 to 200 feet deep these labourers dug the lines by hand while geology and popular culture pushed them forward. At the turn of the century writers like HG Wells were full of ideas about going to the centre of the Earth, digging deep into its' core and in the main part London was built on clay-perfect for tunneling. Except of course for South London, which is mainly not clay, hence the disproportionate look of the Underground map-only 26 Tube stations are South of the River.

With the new Greathead shield work started on the first 'tube" in 1886, two tunnels smaller than expected, and with the trains at first planned to be dragged by steel cables. But before the work was completed the idea of electrification was embraced and so the modern Tube system was born. The name "tube" was actually a slang term amongst Londoners, but clearly so right even Queen Victoria used it and it caught on, despite the first company trying to get Subway adopted as the preferred noun. Londoners decided to leave that to another City across the Atlantic.

The power originally came from a generating station at Stockwell -that was before the construction of the two giant power stations that would power the 20th Century Tubeway one of which is the giant Lots Road station in Fulham, alongside the River and called the "Chelsea Monster" a name shared years later with a player called Mickey Droy.

In the 1890's though the small power station that was Stockwell did not quite have the juice. The further away from base that the trains ran, the less their underpowered engines could pull. Lights flickered and travel was slowed, especially uphill. The passengers sat on long benches, leaning against the sides of the coaches like we do today. Entry and exit was via the end of coach doors onto a small platform where a guard would stand and control a little lattice gate allowing passengers to jump off, or fight their way on-because the trains seemed always crowded.

Mid carriage doors only arrived much later with the advent of air controlled systems, pioneered on the Bakerloo in 1920. The system was pretty much rolled out at the end of the century and the carriages started looking like tube trains. Meanwhile Station names were written on the dimly lit platform walls, but as the carriages had no windows the guard called them out.

There were two drivers per train, and because there was no dead man's handle brake system they both were on standby all the time. The stations had domed ceilings, to allow for space for the lift systems, but today only Kennington Station survives from those times.

Technically those early electric powered trains used the third rail system. Today of course there is a fourth rail.

CITY & SOUTH LONDON RAILWAY LAYOUT OF STOCKWELL STATION & DEPOT, 1890

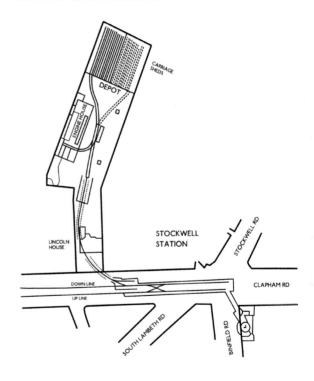

REDRAWN FROM JAMES HENRY GREATHEAD'S ORIGINAL DESIGN
FROM THE MINUTES OF THE PROCEEDINGS OF THE INSTITUTION OF CIVIL ENGINEERS

Chapter 11

The impact of War

The Second World War provided London with some of the most iconic and important moments in its' relationship with the Underground. It also provided us with some of the most enduring images of the Tube and the people it served as the station platforms were transformed into homes for Londoners, a safe haven, a place of refuge, warmth and camaraderie and it created a bond between London and its' Underground that has proved far deeper than any other between a City and its transport system.

However we should not forget the impact the First World War had on both the development of the Underground and importantly, as with other indus-

tries, the role of women.

During the Great War women began increasingly to take up jobs on the system, filling in for absentee staff that had either enlisted or been called away on the home front. When Maida Vale station opened on June 6 1915 it was staffed entirely by women, and by the end of 1917 the Metropolitan Railway had over 550 women working for it.

Furthermore, although not reaching the levels of shelter afforded during the Blitz, when the Zeppelin raids were threatening the capital some 300,000 Londoners sought a refuge from the German bomb raids in the stations on one night-a figure greater than any single night in

the Second War. Aldwych station even provided a sanctuary for many of the paintings from the National Gallery. The lines kept going as well with much bravery from the staff: a marble marker at Baker Street commemorates the 137 employees killed during the war.

With the coming of the Second World War the public naturally assumed that the places they had been encouraged to visit for years (Posters extolled the warm and bright nature of the stations during the 1930's) would provide a haven from the Blitz. But sadly to begin with the authorities were not compliant.

Posters went up forbidding the practice. There was clearly a thought amongst the government that the tubes needed to keep going and were not a location for the masses to sleep. However, evenings brought a mass of people

ABOVE 80 feet below the surface of Piccadilly Circus, art treasures from the Tate Gallery, London Museum and other collections were stored during the Second World War in a disused part of the Underground line, which was sealed off for their safekeeping. Here shown being brought out along the platform at Piccadilly Underground Station, to be returned to their usual resting places

THE IMPACT OF WAR

RIGHT *Underground Railway women at work on London's Tube Network, 1942.*

Rose Pillon offers advice to a passengers from the 'Tickets and Information' window at this London Underground station. Rose worked as a booking clerk during the First World War and returned to this job when war broke out "with the same smiling efficiency".

looking for safety and mainly it was indeed the masses. Those who came were those who needed somewhere to shelter, they were the Londoners who did not have back gardens with huts or shelters of their own or capacious cellars- so naturally they came to the stations and threatened to storm them if they were not allowed down. Many people got round the Tube sheltering ban by buying cheap penny travel tickets and then refused to leave the platforms, others simply made their way onto the platforms through sheer weight of numbers.

So finally the public were reluctantly admitted to the stations with all the deep level tube stations acting as night-time refuges. On 8 October 1940 the government announced the U-turn and ended the unenforceable ban on sheltering in the Tube. By that Christmas the goodwill was restored with London Transport staff distributing over 11,000 toys, presented by America's Air Raid Relief Fund, to children sheltering in stations.

Even then there was a slight suggestion that perhaps this sheltering thing was

the sort of activity that men folk would not join in with, something the was just for women and children. Whatever the case the ferocity of the airborne attack soon changed this mentality, and the tubes became a universal shelter.

Bunks were brought in for the kids and food and drink from catering trains was introduced. Drink was mainly in the form of tea -there were even especially made huge two gallon tea pots, and communal singing, music, dancing and sharing of rations became the norm. Platforms filled up and eventually it became necessary to provide canteens and toilet facilities for those sheltering in the stations. By the end of the war there were over 22,000 beds installed in Underground stations, and over seven tons of food was handed out to those sheltering every night.

Sheltering in a tube station may have given a sense of security but conditions were hardly attractive. Space was limited and many have spoken of the terrible smell of so many people in a confined space without adequate ventilation. With all the bodies, the lack of fresh air and the heat lead inevitably to infections and bugs, mainly those that irritate the skin. Many people became territorial about 'their space' leading to frequent arguments and a cottage industry sorting out who was sleeping where sprang up-although the authorities did their best by providing a "ticker" allocating reserved spaces to stop the black market in sleeping area sales.

Throughout, as the posters proclaimed, "London Transport Carried On" and the first trains of the day acted as an almighty wake up call to the thousands drowsing on the platforms. Of course there were some financial incentives as well as safety for those sheltering: lighting and heating were paid for, and during the height of the Blitz some 177,000 Londoners regularly spent the night Underground-about 4% of the population.

Card games, chess, sing-alongs, and lots of cockney humour provided a special atmosphere that Londoners who remember those evenings and nights speak about with huge fondness. There was a "make do and make the best of it" spirit as people brought deckchairs

and tables, even piano's, down to the platforms, they swaddled the bright lights with cloth to reduce light levels during the sleeping hours, looked after each others' children and organised games for families. They read special

shelter pamphlets and were sketched by artists like Henry Moore who created his famous shelter sketchbooks that are such a brilliant evocation of the scenes under the streets of the stricken City. In short Londoners made the Underground a home from home that has always meant that those deep level stations in particular have become the people's places and have their own special role in popular mythology.

Tragically the tube was not always as safe as those sheltering within had hoped and some of the worst tragedies of the Blitz occurred underground. At Balham Station during the night of 14 October 1940 a huge bomb blew open a water main and sewer which flooded the platforms killing 68 people including four railway staff. Two nights later at Bounds Green a heavy bomb fell directly on the tube station killing sixteen people. In November 1940 one of the cut and cover stations-Sloane Square-was directly hit and 79 people were killed on a train that was just leaving the platform.

At Bank station on January

BELOW A tube station being used as an air raid shelter

11 1941 fifty six people were killed when a bomb blasted through the upper level of the station, sending masonry and concrete onto those sheltering, injuring and killing those below.

The most terrible disaster was at Bethnal Green, a station not even in operation at the end of the Central Line. The station had yet to be fully opened but it was acting as a shelter. After reports of a particularly heavy attack on Berlin one night Londoners knew that in the vicious war of tit for tat the City was bound to get hit really hard the following night. That next evening when a new anti aircraft gun started firing nearby with an extra loud sound that many were not accustomed to, there was a sense of panic that the imminent major attack was about to come. Crowds swelled at the small staircase running down to the platform. Tragically a mother and child stumbled and fell at the foot of the stairs and the crowd poured over them, hundreds fell, hundreds were crushed by the crowds and the weight of humanity. One hundred and seventy three people were killed, of which, awfully, sixty were children. A further ninety were badly injured. It was the worst civilian disaster of the entire war. The full cause and extent of the tragedy was not revealed until after 1945, a detrimental effect on morale was feared. But the East End knew all about it, too many families were deeply affected and even today

BELOW Two Dutch sailors and a Dutch soldier descend the steps into a London Underground 'Tube' station on an evening out in London, 1940

there are Londoners who will not use the station. The supreme irony was that on that night not a single Nazi bomb fell on London.

Away from the stations eight purpose built deep tunnels were dug to afford extra protection and shelter. One was used to plan D-day, another as Eisenhower's London hideaway. Today they are used mainly as storage facilities. An abandoned station at Down Street was transformed into a back up cabinet war room, and while Churchill's lair off Downing Street was being prepared it acted as his nighttime h.q. during 1940. Some say they can still smell the roast dinner and cigars that the pm survived on.

Elsewhere Brompton Road station on the Piccadilly line, which was closed in 1934, was converted into an underground Operations Room for London's anti-aircraft control.

In practical terms the Underground had to change with the coming of war as well. The rapid expansion of the Underground services into London's suburbs throughout the 30s were brought abruptly to a halt with the outbreak of War. It then swung into high action with its central role in helping to evacuate children and expectant mothers from London to the countryside in 1939. Within a couple of days of the outbreak, London Transport successfully evacuated 600,000 vulnerable Londoners.

During the war, signs warning passengers to carry their gas marks were on display at every Underground station and despite a ban on geographic transport maps during the war, the Tube map was still permitted, presumably because it wouldn't have been much help to Nazi paratroopers.

As the war finally drew to a close the whole system seemed to be full to busting, with American GI's swelling the crowds alongside homecoming troops. But even if the lack of maintenance during the war years, the wear and tear created by the bombing, the weight of people using the stations 24/7 and the lack of money to renovate the tube might have left the Underground feeling down it was far from out. Vitally the system was now seen, more than ever, as the people's friend.

LEFT *Underground Railway women at work on London's Tube Network, 1942.*

Miss Feely operates one of the large lifts which carry passengers from street level down to the platforms and back up to the street again. Before the war, Miss Feely was a barmaid. Note the posters on display behind her: one provides the public with 'Seven facts about war saving' and the other is an advertisement for the Gaumont State cinema, revealing that "My Favourite Blonde" starring Bob Hope and "Saboteur" are currently playing.

Chapter 12

The City and South London and the "Drain"

Remember James Greathead, the engineer behind that shield digging idea? Well he was not just a dusty engineer he was also quite an entrepreneur and in 1884 he was part of a group that proposed a new line termed the City of London & Southwark Subway.

Note the use of subway-they mean a tube, but wanted it well lit, modern, a step forward from the dirty cut and cover lines with their smut and smoke and were keen to show the difference.

The line as proposed would run from the Elephant and Castle to just north of London Bridge, King William Street, and really this was the first proper Tube-even if it was a bit small.

It had two tunnels (dug using those shields of course) an up and down line in separate "tubes" it had single class carriages, electrically lit, with room for standing and like many fellow lines it failed to cover the cost of construction.

What is remarkable is that it became the first electrically operated line. After initially aiming to be cable drawn, by 1890 it was ready to go, with a burst of confidence and optimism the line renamed itself City and South London and pushed on to Clapham via Kennington, Oval and Stockwell. So it was a double first-the first electric and the first one class railway in Britain. Incidentally the technology used can still be seen today in Brighton where a railway the system

ABOVE Borough station on the City and South London Railway, 1890

was based on devised by electric pioneer Magnus Volk still runs along the sea front in Kemp Town (near the nudist beach if this excitement on its own is not enough).

The carriages were small and low and long, with padded benches ranged against the walls. The tunnels were small as well but the ambitions behind the line were big. It pushed on and Northwards towards Bank eventually getting there in 1900 by which time another line had got

there too-the so-called Drain.

The Waterloo & City Railway to give the line its' correct name was created as a subsidiary of the LSWR to allow main-line passengers to reach the City. It was given its permission to burrow after the flurry of applications in 1892. At this time Parliament laid down some rules- tunnels had to be a certain minimum size of 11ft diameter and guidelines concerning the treatment of freeholders that you tunneled under

ABOVE City & South London Railway train. Print from Illustrated London News, 8 November 1890

were prescribed. But undeterred the railways lines continued.

The Waterloo and City is probably the simplest line on the system, just a connection between Waterloo and Bank-and this simplicity is reflected in the name people have always used for it-the drain.

It is just one and half miles long, easily the shortest, and takes just four minutes to travel. The Drain is the only line to be entirely underground and was one of the simplest to build. Trains were taken down there by means of a lift, there is a big grated hole at the back of Waterloo that they can be elevated through, and the name Drain-well that comes not from the fact that the line is susceptible to rain water because it is not, but it does have a large amount of seepage-every day-from the river.

It is unashamedly commuter bias, there is no hotel at Waterloo unlike every other main station in town, the idea is to use the Drain to go to and from work and then get off home to the suburbs. From the beginning the Bank end of the line had a really long incline and therefore a long tiring walk to reach the surface as the City authorities would not allow a surface building for a lift. In 1960 though, there came some relief when the first two trav-o-lators were installed. Both walkways run the same way in the morning i.e. uphill, although in the evening they alternate in direc-tion. The engineer for the walking pave-ment was incidentally a Mr. Drain. At weekends when the City sleeps so does the line. There is no service when there are no commuters.

The line remained in Rail ownership until 1994 when it was sold to London Underground for £1.

Chapter 13

The Central Line

The Central London Railway was formed in 1891 to build a tube railway along the east-west axis of London, connecting the western suburbs to the City. The line, which opened in 1900, ran straight along Oxford Street and its extensions to each end - Bayswater Road and High Holborn. It too had been born by the provisions of 1892 and for the main part was a disciplined exercise.

The tubes were actually dug on top of each other, rather than side by side, to allow both to run squarely under the road and avoid private housing. Again the syndicate included Greathead (although he died before completion) and of course his shields were employed

again in the digging, which started in 1896.

There was plenty of American money behind the line as well, so carriages were "cars", the line ran eastbound and westbound (not "up" and "down") and there were leather straps a la New York. The license allowed expansion to Liverpool Street in the East and Shepherds Bush in the West, and in 1900 it opened. Twelve years later Liverpool Street was reached.

At Bank the platform curves quite radically which means there was an urgent need for those "Mind the Gap' announcements,

The Central was one class and the line

quickly became known as the Tuppeny tube. And yes in this case the word Tube was actually encouraged, written large above the stations. The Central felt modern, the electric lights in the cars glowed brightly with no voltage drop-there were relay stations all along the line, and the cars themselves were elegantly attired…well thick cushions anyway.

Two problems came to the fore; the first was that parts of the line, smelled rather odd. The solution was simple; hundreds of electric fans were installed. The other problem was vibration: the line used electric locomotives for a short time, but problems with excessive shaking caused them to be replaced by multiple-unit stock. There were also two steam locos, used mostly in the depots to

ABOVE A postcard for the Central London Railway (now the London Underground's Central line) showing a train at Bank station the electric driver's motor car, circa 1903

allow stock to be moved without using power rails. Later some of the electric locos were fitted with trolley poles to draw power from overhead wires in the depots. This modification allowed draughtsmen on the surface to draw straight lines, as they had been the main complainants about the vibration.

The line was still known at the Tuppeny tube, especially by the Daily Mail, even when it raised the fare to 3d, but then why let the facts get in the way. There was a separate ticket office in Selfridges, although the line did resist the overtures of the store to call the station Selfridges rather than Bond Street with a tunnel directly into the department store. The exception to this naming rule came when Herbert Chapman, then the manager of London's most successful team at the time, suggested that Gillespie Road should have a new name-and it did... Arsenal. While on the subject, there is of course no Chelsea station-just Fulham Broadway, which must irk, especially as it is immortalised by Ian Dury's What a Waste when he sings, "I could be the ticket man at Fulham Broadway Station". They don't have a cottage by the river either but that is another story.

The line was called the Central London Railway when it opened, but when London Transport took it over the name changed to the Central London line in 1933 and in 1937 became what we know today-the Central Line. It was originally a sort of pastel orange on the maps but in 1934 it went red, and has stayed that way.

FAR LEFT A poster for the Central London Railway (now the London Underground's Central line) extolling the ease of the railway's use, 1905

LEFT Passengers read to pass the time on the journey home from work aboard a Central Line train

Chapter 14

The Northern Line

The Northern was yet another line to be created out of those authorised in 1892, but really was an elaborate combination of some existing, and some new builds. The syndicate behind it again had our friend James Henry Greathead, together with his shield, on board.

The plan was for a line running from the main line station at Finsbury Park to Drayton Park, where it would go underground and then run in twin tunnels to Moorgate, so yet another line bringing in commuters to the City.

Unfortunately though once up and running the line was largely a failure to begin with. There were beautiful carriages that

felt oversize with lots of wood, clocks and room. Crucially though passenger figures were about a third of estimates and the losses piled up.

In 1912 the line was bought by the Underground Electric Railways Company of London who wanted to extend the Northern further south. They re-introduced the idea of classes on the train with both first and third class seats offered.

ABOVE Underground sign at Belsize Park station

LEFT London Underground Northern Line 1995 tube stock electric multiple unit 51705 at Finchley Central tube station

Meanwhile the Charing Cross, Euston and Hampstead Railway was opened in 1907 running from Charing Cross via Euston and Camden Town up to Golders Green and Highgate. In 1913 it too was taken over by the Underground Electric Railways Company of London.

This is why to this day the line is complicated with two Northern branches, two central branches and the Southern branch-it's really three lines and a signaling nightmare.

The joining process largely took place in the 1920's, first in the north. Then in 1926 the two parts in the south were nipped together, with Waterloo added in for good measure and extra customers. The deep tube running south was much needed, and hugely over subscribed even at the start. It was the longest in the world at 17.5 miles and reached all the way down to Morden. It was not until 1937 that it gained the title Northern Line.

The stations, especially on the line up to Golders Green are deep. Very deep. Hampstead Station takes the biscuit with the deepest lift at 181 feet, and the systems deepest point below ground is just a little to the North of the station below Hampstead Heath at 221 feet.

Now the Northern line is the busiest on the network and it was the first to use lifts. Every year over 207 million passengers use the Northern line over its 36 miles of track and 50 stations. It is a colossus but a flawed giant with an illogical and unplanned history but somehow it works, and of course the architecture of some of its stations is very special.

FAR LEFT "Golders Green" a poster from the Underground Electric Railways Company of London (UERL) advertising the benefits of living in Golders Green, the northern terminus of the recently opened Charing Cross, 1908

LEFT The nickname "Tube" comes from the almost circular tube-like tunnels through which the small profile trains travel. This photograph shows a northbound Northern Line train leaving a tunnel mouth just north of Hendon Central station

Chapter 15

The East London Line

RIGHT To the right is the Brunel Museum and to the left is the Rotherhithe Shaft of the Thames Tunnel. In the middle distance beyond the garages is the roof of Rotherhithe Underground Station on the East London Line

Now if ever a line could be described as the runt of the pack then it is this one. If ever a line could have a complex about whether it is underground or overground then the same applies, because over the years it has fluctuated between the two. It also has yet another very colourful character nestling in its early history.

The East London actually opened way back in 1869 between Wapping and New Cross with a connection to the London, Brighton and South Coast Railway. The plan was to link the main line stations north and south of the river using the Brunel tunnel under the Thames as its main connection to the south (that was the tunnel that used Brunel's shield not Greathead). But poor connections especially in the north meant the link was less than brilliant and serious financial problems followed.

The financial problems sat pretty squarely in the lap of one Albert Grant who was a financier for whom the term colourful was a compliment. He was "very inventive" let's say...and he used the equivalent of junk email, the penny post, to inveigle small investors all across Britain to put their savings into his schemes. These enterprises always seemed to be exotic, difficult to pin down and promised tremendous returns. There was the Cadiz Waterworks, the Labuan Coal Company and the Emma Silver Mine in his port-

folio. Locations of the investments were often a mystery or vague at best, but what was certain was that people's investment had a habit of shrinking fast. Grant got a cool £1million pumped into Emma Silver Mining but pretty soon it was worth just a four hundredth of that. Grant made £100,000 in commission on that one.

Albert insisted that his staff should call him Baron Grant, asserting that he had been given the title in Italy after raising some money for building a row of shops. His flotation and fund raising for the East London Line had the same result as some of the earlier ventures. It was a confidence bubble and the money vanished.

The little line had no stock of its own, using the trains of other operators and was really an overground rail link with freight and consumer traffic sharing the lines. So unlike any of the others, the East London Line is the only Underground line that was planned and built as a main-line railway.

The East London also had spurs added to it connecting Aldgate and Tower, the Met and the District, and for many years trains ran to a range of destinations south of the river, such as Croydon, Addiscombe Road, and even Brighton, as well as to a separate terminus at New Cross. Coal was carried on the line, military hardware was shunted through the tunnel, so it was part underground, part main line rail, part passenger and part freight. It was also part surface, part cut and cover and part tube. Talk about an identity crisis.

So not only was the line broke but had a failed and tarnished attempt at fund raising behind it, so enter Sir Edward Watkin who bought it for a song, restored its finances and managed to incorporate it into the network of railways that were all chaired by him thus saving its' bacon.

In 1933 it came under the control of London Transport and was officially marked purple on the map-the same as the Metropolitan and described as Metropolitan Line-East London Section and a little white line down the middle was added which has actually remained until today. But as the docks faded so did the usage of the line. In the 1980's it was allowed to become a fully fledged tube line in its own right and coloured orange (on the outside) on the tube map, but the independence was short lived, and having no entry into zone 1 it was bound to be isolated.

In 1995 came closure for work on the leaking tunnel and for something to be done about the terrible smell the Evening Standard had described for years. But the work took ages with a row about how important it was to keep the visual appearance of the tunnel (it became a conservation issue…you know the sort of thing, planners were involved). When the line re-opened in 1998 Wapping, the oldest station on the system, continued to smell and sound like it was in the middle of a massive waterworks, but the leak was cured and the line had gained a connection to the Jubilee line at the new station Canada Water.

Best of all in 2010 the London Overground (the rail equivalent of the North Circular Road, this was the line that picked its way from West to East

London via Brondesbury, Kensal Rise and Gospel Oak amongst others) incorporated the East London so the line was back from the underground to the above surface world. Connecting right across the upper reaches of the map and also integrating well with the DLR the East London line-still coloured orange-is now a revelation, a part of a great service with great aesthetics and a speedier ethos than the old Richmond-Stratford line. The runt has grown up.

BELOW Shoreditch Station (Sep '08) The former northern terminus of London Underground's East London Line lies abandoned and derelict. Behind the station building is the new steel bridge that will carry the East London Line (as part of the London Overground) over the Liverpool Street line to Shoreditch High Street and onto Dalston

Chapter 16

The Piccadilly Line

Like the Northern the Piccadilly line was another example of a network created by fusing together some existing lines with some new tunneling and a bit of re-direction and extension. Also like the Northern the Piccadilly was essentially part of Yerkes' great scheme, although he did not live to see any of it materialise.

The original Piccadilly Line - from Finsbury Park to Hammersmith - was formed by merging three separate proposals. From east to west, these were:

THE GREAT NORTHERN & STRAND RAILWAY, from Wood Green to Aldwych, located underneath the GNR main line between Wood Green and King's Cross.

THE BROMPTON & PICCADILLY CIRCUS RAILWAY, from Air Street (near Piccadilly Circus) to a point near South Kensington.

THE DEEP LEVEL DISTRICT, a proposal by the Metropolitan District Railway to build an express tube under its line from just east of Earl's Court to Mansion House, with an intermediate station at Embankment; electric locos would take over from steam trains at Earl's Court.

The District purchased the B&PCR in 1898. In 1901 the Yerkes Group took over all three companies before any construction had been started and combined the three proposals into the

Great Northern, Piccadilly & Brompton Railway (though in day-to-day use this was quickly abbreviated to the Piccadilly Railway.)

But there was another predatory American on the prowl and Yerkes had to fight off JP Morgan in the shape of Morgan's son who was propounding a

scheme called Morgan's tube. He was well backed but he had not figured on Yerkes' cunning who exploited a gap in the shareholders to get his own way.

The result was that the Great Northern and Strand Railway was combined with the Brompton and Piccadilly. Digging started in 1902.

ABOVE A northbound London Underground 1973 stock EMU arrives at Covent Garden on the Piccadilly Line

At the eastern end of the line there were problems though as the overground railway (in the shape of the GNR) considered the territory beyond Finsbury Park their own. They did not want any suggestion of their customers being seduced off the railways and onto the Tube before they had reached London. Therefore when they agreed to hand over the route to Yerkes, they retained ownership of the tube station (under their main-line one) and demanded a veto over any extension northwards.

In that way Finsbury Park became the end of the line and the scene of increasing congestion. But despite pressure over the next decade or so, the GNR and its successor the LNER were unrelenting.

By 1923 Frank Pick had risen to Assistant Managing Director of the Underground group, the company that had grown from Yerkes' association. Pick could see how bad the congestion at Finsbury Park was, and he would not be denied-he realised he could exploit public opinion. Pick set about taking some illustrative pictures-all photographed at the times of the greatest crush-and released them to the Press.

The result was an outcry in favour of extending the line. Combine that clamour to rising unemployment amongst industrial workers and the tide was overwhelming. The new line would bring new work and cure a crowding problem-the answer was obvious.

Pick's plan involved pushing northwards to Cockfosters, and Westwards alongside the District Line from Hammersmith with faster trains calling at Acton, Hounslow and Uxbridge. Fifteen stations would be rebuilt and in just three years from 1930 the work was complete.

The stations include some of the most elegant architecturally and rather than rob the overground of customers the line seemed to create its' own passenger base. New houses sprang up and the resulting crowded suburbs can be seen with 30's semi's standing in their estates alongside late Victorian terraces and Edwardian detached houses which had come with the original overground.

Now of course the modern Piccadilly goes all the way to Heathrow linking all the terminals and while this works really well for day trippers and workers, the lack of large baggage storage on the tube trains does confuse incomers from the US or India with their enormous suitcases forced into a corner of the carriage. Perhaps the Heathrow Express needs a rethink as New Yorkers heading for the West End seem reluctant to use the service when it takes them to Paddington, where they have to get another tube or taxi. In all the Piccadilly carries about 75 million passengers a year, with 52 stations on the 44 miles of track it runs.

As a side note there was a small addition to the Piccadilly, the Aldwych branch, which was called, glamorously, the Theatre Express. It only really became the express for three years from 1907 and then only in the evenings. The idea was that it would take elegant theatregoers home to Finsbury Park and beyond after the shows. But beyond Finsbury Park is probably not the home of an enormous and avid group of culture vultures so the idea stalled.

The line was essentially just a shuttle service, an offshoot not connected to anywhere else and in 1994 it was closed. The Aldwych tube station was shut, but just before being abandoned it had its origi-nal name-Strand-restored. Most recently my old friend Michel Morris (who was responsible for those arty hi-jackings of BBC Radio 4 recently, some featuring Underground sound effects) has hired the station for some experimental and highly creative events, punctuated by announcements of Mind the Gap and Tickets Please. It is also the most used of the "ghost stations" as a film or TV filming location.

BELOW Aldwych tube station looking north towards Holborn, shortly before closure on 30 September 1994

Chapter 17

Disasters

The Underground has a remarkably safe record considering the huge number of passengers, the frequency of journeys and the proximity of people, mechanical engineering, speed and the overall sense of confinement.

Some of the worst disasters were acts of war, and the most terrible civilian tragedy-although not caused by a bomb-was during the Second World War at Bethnal Green and can be read about elsewhere but accidents, collisions and terrorism have taken their toll as well. This is in addition to the many labourers, engineers and builders who lost their lives in constructing the network.

The first accidents on the underground

occurred within a couple of months of opening in 1863 just slow-moving collisions at Farringdon Street station. But it was not until 1938 that the first passenger deaths occurred as a result of a crash. On May 17 a signaling failure at Charing Cross lead to a District line accident. Six people died and a further 45 people were injured when an eastbound Circle line train ploughed into the back of a train in the tunnels between Charing Cross and Temple. The passengers on the Ealing-Barking train, which was stationary, were largely unhurt but the carnage was considerable especially given the mainly wooden composition of the carriages.

At the end of the war in December 1945 a Metropolitan line train traveling from

SITE OF THE WORST CIVILIAN DISASTER
OF THE SECOND WORLD WAR

IN MEMORY OF
173 MEN, WOMEN AND CHILDREN
WHO LOST THEIR LIVES ON THE
EVENING OF WEDNESDAY 3RD MARCH 1943
DESCENDING THESE STEPS TO BETHNAL GREEN
UNDERGROUND AIR RAID SHELTER

NOT FORGOTTEN

Baker Street to Aylesbury in thick fog crashed into the back of the Aldgate to Watford service between Northwood and Northwood Hill stations. The train had previously passed a red signal while following 'stop and proceed' rules, which allow drivers to continue slowly through a red light after having waited for at least a minute. The collision crushed the

rear two carriages of the Watford train together, but it was not the impact that inflicted the fatalities.

The wreckage caught fire due to electrical arcing from the power rails. Three people died of smoke inhalation, but meanwhile around 500 passengers had to be detrained from the two trains involved in

ABOVE Memorial plaque commemorating the victims of an accident on the southeastern staircase of Bethnal Green tube station during an air raid alert in 1943

brakes shortly afterwards under the semi-conscious impression that he had reached the station. However, the train had not stopped, but was instead traveling at 12mph, leading it to continue through the sand drag, over the buffers and into a wall at the terminus. The driver died due to his illness while stuck inside the carriage, but nobody else was seriously hurt. Now technological improvements have made that sort of accident impossible.

Far worse was the accident at Stratford, which is probably one of the unluckiest stations on the system. In all Stratford has had three serious accidents, all accountable to signaling problems. On 5 December 1947, a signal failure on the Central line meant that trains running on that section of line had to follow 'stop and proceed' rules. However, a train carrying just three signalling staff sent to investigate the cause of the failure crashed into the back of the empty train in front of it at a speed of around 10mph, trapping the driver and the signal staff in the cab, with one of the men dying before they could be rescued.

the crash and another which had arrived from the other direction, with passengers having to cross live power rails to escape the site of the accident. The current was only switched off thirteen minutes after the fire had started so that firemen could dowse the wreckage with water.

The following year on 30 July, 1946, a driver applying the brakes on a train approaching Edgware station on the Northern line suffered from a coronary thrombosis, leading him to release the

Six years later and a similar accident took place but with far more serious consequences. On 8 April 1953, again signal failures led to delays on the Central line, with drivers again following 'stop and proceed' rules. However, a train heading eastbound towards Epping ploughed into the back of a stationary train waiting in the tunnel between Stratford and Leyton just before 7pm. The accident left twelve passengers dead and many wounded. The driver was hurt but survived and was later charged with having ignored the 'stop and proceed' rules by a Public Inquiry.

A third accident occurred just west of Stratford on 24 January 1979, just after signal failures prompted an investigation on the open-air section of line west of the station. Following the 'stop and proceed' rules, a train containing passengers headed slowly along the westbound line so that a technician on board could look for faults in the wiring. A second passenger train then ran into the back of the first, injuring a handful of passengers. Once more the cause was a lack of caution when proceeding through a red light, and the driver of the second train was given the blame for the accident.

Away from Stratford at Bromley by Bow in 1955, after having been stranded for 2½

hours at a point uphill from the station due to the electricity being off over much of the east part of the District line, a driver was allowed to run his train into the station under gravity alone. This caused a problem though. The air brakes used on trains at the time required electric motors to maintain the pressure, and so the lack of electric power meant only the handbrake could be used to control the train's speed. Having released the pressure in the airbrakes, the driver found that the train was moving but he could not stop it with just the handbrake, the train ran down the track and crashed at around 5mph into an empty train at Bromley by Bow station. 44 passengers were hurt; fortunately no one was seriously injured.

On 28 July 1958, a fire started in the electrical wiring of a Central line train between Shepherd's Bush and Holland Park station in west London, with most of the passengers suffering from smoke inhalation and one person later dying from breathing the fumes. A similar incident occurred two years later on 12 August 1960 when a fire started in the front carriage of a train between Redbridge and Gants Hill for the same reason. Fortunately no one was killed, as

LEFT Memorial at Bethnal Green Underground Station. Wreathes of poppies and a few words of explanation have been fixed to these railings immediately adjacent to the steps leading into Bethnal Green underground station by campaigners for a fitting memorial to those who lost their lives in the disaster in 1943 when a crowd became crushed when entering the station to shelter from an air raid

the train was only partially full, though a few dozen people were taken to hospital.

But worse was to come. On 28 February 1975 the most terrible tube accident in living memory took place. The images and the memory of that crash have lived on in the public mind ever since. Forty-three people were killed when a train arriving at Moorgate station simply accelerated into the tunnel, hit the sand drag, smashed the buffer and thundered into the concrete wall at the end of the line. It was an awful and total disaster and there was only one person to blame.

There was no evidence of malfunction on the train or track and the driver, Leslie Newson, was seen conscious and healthy at the controls seconds before the impact.

It took four days for the police, ambulance men, and over 1,300 officers of the fire brigade to remove the dead and dying from the wreckage. Leslie Newson's body was the last to be recovered. Two enquiries were set up, and both immediately agreed there was nothing wrong with the train or the track. The guard was innocent of malpractice and even if he had been totally aware of what was happening he could have done nothing.

The evidence seemed to suggest that Newson, a veteran of Dunkirk, was a creature of habit and totally reliable. He had planned a holiday to the USA, was about to buy a new car, was looking forward to a transfer back to the depot he preferred…but as he entered the station witnesses said he did not even lift his hands to protect himself as the train reached the end of the line. The only explanation was that he was responsible for the terrible crash. The Coroners' jury returned a verdict of accidental death on all the victims, including the driver.

TERRORISM

During the IRA bombing campaign of the 1970s, there were two major explosions on the Underground, both of which took place in 1976. There had been some fortunate escapes before that. Two bombs had been planted at Baker Street tube in August 1973 but both were found and defused, while another was planted at Sloane Square on Boxing Day that year and did nothing except destroy a telephone kiosk. A large bomb was also found in a case at Oxford Circus in

February 1976 and was defused, while another exploded on an empty train outside Cannon Street, injuring a handful of passengers on an adjacent train.

The first major explosion occurred on 15 March, 1976 on a Hammersmith & City line train just west of West Ham when a bomber realised his package, which had begun to smoke, was about to explode and hurled it along the carriage, escaping through the driver's cab. Nine people were injured by the 5lb bomb but sadly the heroic driver, who bravely pursued the terrorist, was shot dead alongside an engineer who also lost his life. The bomber was eventually cornered by the police and shot himself. The following day, a second bomb exploded on a train reversing into the siding at Wood Green. No one was badly hurt, but had the bomb gone off ten minutes later it would have caught a train full of supporters heading home from Arsenal station.

Another wave of IRA bombs came in the early 1990s, starting in February 1991 with a litterbin bomb outside Victoria station. The bomb killed one man and injured many others, as the warning given by the IRA had not left enough time for

evacuation of the station. To help prevent any further attacks, the litterbins were removed from all Underground stations and have never returned.

BELOW Newspaper headlines at Waterloo station around 15.00 hours on July 7 2005

In August the same year, three incendiary devices were discovered on the undercarriage of a train at Hammersmith, and in December bombs exploded on trains at Harrow-on-the-Hill station and Neasden depot, though no one was hurt in either case. The following year the IRA placed devices on several trains, though most were found and defused, with one device exploding at Barking. The only major attack came in April 1993 when a fertiliser bomb weighing around a ton was detonated in Bishopsgate, destroying the Underground station and wrecking surrounding buildings.

7/7

The worst act of terror on the Underground was nothing to do with the Irish troubles though. The attack came on July 7 2005 when commuters at 8.50am were subjected to a quadruple simultaneous onslaught, three bombs on the Underground all within 50 seconds of each other and a fourth on board a bus by Tavistock Square about an hour later.

Two of the train bombs were on the Circle line, at Aldgate seven people died from their injuries, a further six people died at Edgware Road, while 26 people died between Russell Square and Kings Cross on the Piccadilly. The bus bomb claimed a further 13 lives. All of the suicide bombers were killed.

There were over 770 injured victims of the action. The victims on the Piccadilly line were almost double those lost on the Circle line, as the blast was less restricted there as it was a cut and cover line. In the confines of the deep tube system the word "terror" barely describes the horrendous scenes.

Unlike the past incidents involving the IRA, the 7/7 bombings led to much ini-

In memory of those who were killed in the bomb attack on a Piccadilly line train between King's Cross St. Pancras and Russell Square stations on 7th July 2005

James Adams   Arthur Frederick   Helen Katherine Jones   Mihaela Otto
Philip Beer   Karolina Gluck   Susan Levy   Atiq Sharifi
Anna Brandt   Gamze Gunoral   Shelley Mather   Ihab Slimane
Ciaran Cassidy   Ojara Ikeagwu   Michael Matsushita   Christian Njoya Diawara Small
Rachelle Chung For Yuen   Emily Jenkins   James Mayes   Monika Suchocka
Liz Daplyn   Adrian Johnson   Behnaz (Nazy) Mozakka   Mala Trivedi
Sam Badham   Lee Christopher Harris

London will not forget them and all those who suffered that day

tial nervousness about returning to the tube, with most trains being almost completely deserted on the day after the explosions. The heightened nervousness was worsened two weeks later with a copycat attack, but fortunately the second round of bombs failed to detonate properly, leading to no loss of life and the 21 July suspects were all later caught by the police. Tragically the alarming panic and suspicion throughout the system during the bombings and their aftermath led to an incident where the Brazilian Jean Charles de Menezes was shot on a train after being wrongly identified as a terror suspect. It was a stark demonstration of the vulnerability of society to these attacks and how the lines of justice and everything else we hold dear are sorely stretched by these acts, which are so hard to understand.

ABOVE Plaque at Russell Square station in memory of those killed in the 7/7 bombings

LEFT Ambulances at Russell Square, London after the 7th July bombings

FIRE

As has been seen the huge enemy of safety down in the Underground is fire. Looking back with the advantage of time it seems inconceivable that it took so long to ban smoking from the Tube - it took a terrible disaster with a tragic loss of life to provoke that.

In 1984 at Oxford Circus the writing was on the wall. While building work improving the system was underway the materials used were stored in a closed off passage between the Bakerloo and Victoria line platforms. During the evening on November 23 1984 with passengers heading home a fire started there and swept through the north-bound platform leading to many passengers being taken to hospital with inhalation problems. It could have been so much worse.

The cause was narrowed down to a cigarette and as a result smoking was banned in all subways, platforms, ticket halls and passageways below ground along with the existing ban on smoking actually on the trains. But that was not enough.

On the evening of 18 November, 1987, a small fire due to a dropped ciga-

rette end began on the escalator leading up from the Northern and Piccadilly lines at King's Cross station, igniting the years of accumulation of fluff, human hair, and general rubbish that lay beneath. Although a passenger reported the fire the seriousness of the danger was not fully appreciated. Few steps were taken apart from the calling of four pumps from the local fire brigades.

By the time the fire brigade arrived they instantly needed to get more help. The ticket hall into which the escalators from both the Victoria and the Northern and Piccadilly lines were feeding passengers was now filling with smoke, meanwhile the downward escalators were still operating and dropping thousands into the heart of the danger but now their exit route was blocked.

Brave fire officers were actually escorting passengers up and through the thick smoke towards the exits when a fireball rose up and devastated the escape route killing 31 people. The scenes were terrible, a complete living nightmare.

The issue at the Public Inquiry which followed was not the banning of smoking materials, that smoking ban now extended to all areas of public transport, but the removal of anything that could burn to produce fumes or act as fuel in the event of a fire, along with the installation of sensitive fire detection systems.

The destruction and loss of life caused by the King's Cross fire led to many changes over the next couple of years, making the Underground as safe as humanly possible from 1990 onwards. What a price to pay though for such a seemingly obvious course of action. Smoking on the Tubes now seems as distant a memory as steam trains.

Chapter 18

The Victoria Line

The Victoria line was born in 1968 and is a child of its time: modern, efficient and fast with an idealist slant. The line was created out of plans to relieve congestion- around Finsbury Park naturally as it is the epicenter of all congestion-but also to include the growing populations of the Lea Valley on one side of town and the deep south of Brixton and Stockwell on the other and link them into London's fastest growing workplace of the 60's -the Swinging West End.

The first plan appeared in 1937. The basic idea was for a new express tube line that would run from Victoria to Finsbury Park via stations at Piccadilly Circus, Tottenham Court Road, and Camden Town.

In 1939 this was expanded into plans for an express tube that would be built in three stages. The first stage would run from Morden to Victoria with two intermediate stations, at Tooting Broadway and Clapham Common. Stage 2 would continue to Finsbury Park, but now via Green Park, Bond Street, Great Portland Street, and Camden Town. From there, the third stage would involve two branches northwards.

After World War II, a 1946 plan for London envisaged providing a completely separate express route under the Northern Line, allowing the Victoria and Finsbury Park route (now called "route 8") to serve new markets.

In 1949 the two plans were merged, under the name "route C". Parliamentary powers were finally sought in 1954. The line would only run from Walthamstow to Victoria initially, but two separate southward extensions were intended.

Though the route was decided and Parliament had approved it, the line was now stuck for lack of finance. Opposition of course came from the Tory car lobby- this was the age when the car was king, one MP even suggested spending the money on off street car parking instead, others wanted privately run trains.

So savings were made on the "C" by abandoning the connection at Walthamstow Wood Street, instead terminating the line in tubes at Walthamstow Central, and by adopting new, cheaper, tunneling techniques (tested along the route in 1960). Finally, in 1965 - just in time to keep to the building schedule, authority was given to extend the route to Brixton, with the last minute addition of Pimlico station. Now they needed the money.

Two developments finally allowed the go ahead, the first was the slow down in the economy which meant that public

ABOVE Victoria Station

spending to get things going was seen as a good thing, especially as the chairman of London Transport, Sir John Elliot, explained to the Government that components of the tunnel could be made in the North East and brought down to London thus boosting industry in the North and construction in the South.

The second bit of luck was that two important academics published a hugely

claims on behalf of good transport links.

So with the economic argument won London Transport pushed ahead with the first new line to be built for sixty years. Naming it was a problem though. At first they tried for an amalgam name- like the Bakerloo- but could only come up with the KingVic (which apart from sounding like a pub was felt inappropriate) or strangely the Viking line, which sounds like a cruise operator.

The third suggestion- the Walvic line - just doesn't need any explanation as to why it was rejected, it is just plain ridiculous. The name "Victoria Line" was the brainwave of David McKenna, London Transport's chief commercial officer who went on to become a big cheese in Southern Railways and, taking a diversion into opera, the chairman of the board at Sadler's Wells.

On September 1 1968 the line was opened between Walthamstow and Highbury, then onto Warren Street and Victoria at which point Her Majesty the Queen took the controls of a train to officially declare the line open on March 7 1969. HM also took time to put a 5d

influential piece of work pointing out the enormous economic advantages of improved infrastructure, specifically quantifying the gains to existing transport links by removing undue congestion (meaning the rest of the network, the trains and the roads, yes look roads!) These academics also stressed the social gains implicit. They accepted that the ticket money alone would not repay the investment but the overall benefit to the economy, the time saved by the workforce and so on, would be huge-something that ensuing governments did not always agree with. It was a throw back to the days of Pearson and the altruistic

(2p) ticket into an automatic ticket barrier the first of it's kind, which "read" the ticket and let her through.

Of course she did not really drive the train, but then no one does on the Victoria. The drivers enter their compartment via the carriage as the train is semi automatic so the security is a bit tighter on their cab, they start the train after going through some security checks, and once button A has been pressed the automatic systems on the rail side do the rest. There were rumours some time later that the automatic system worked so well that LT put waxwork dummies into the drivers' cabs to give the illusion someone was driving, but no one mentioned that rumour to the Queen who filled the drivers' position excellently.

Right from the start the Victoria has been a hit. In the first year it carried a third more passengers than estimated and Victoria Station is the busiest in the entire network with Kings Cross and Oxford Circus not far behind. Frequently the Oxford Circus ticket area has to be closed to allow the crowds of commuters and Top Shop customers to die down before re-opening and Victoria's ticket hall is desperate for an overhaul and enlargement, which is happening. Business has always been good on the Victoria line.

The service is super fast with decent gaps between the stations allowing the trains to get up to 50 mph. All the stations have connections-except for poor old Pimlico, which is a Johnny no friends in this respect-and it succeeds in doing what was promised: the Victoria line whisks people in from the suburbs and gets you across Town faster than any other line.

Some find the 60's styling austere, like a Tower block, it is short on natural light, but that clean light blue line is a winner, there are no guards, it could be lonely down there BUT the Victoria is full of people and the tiles have pictures on them even if they are a bit irrelevant. The main thing is that for the last few decades the Victoria has been the star turn on the underground, it is fast and efficient and after a chug round on the District, or a potter on the Northern the commuter is delighted to be conveyed at speed towards Victoria and home to the South coast.

Chapter 19

The Jubilee Line

RIGHT A change of name at Trafalgar Square. This photograph was taken on the southbound Bakerloo Line platform at Trafalgar Square Underground station, just three days before the opening of the Jubilee line on 1 May 1979. On that day, Strand (Northern Line) and Trafalgar Square (Bakerloo Line) would both be re-named Charing Cross and would give interchange with the new Jubilee Line station of the same name. On the same date, the erstwhile Charing Cross stations on the District, Northern and Bakerloo Lines would all be re-named Embankment

The Jubilee line is definitely a line of two halves, and the football metaphor does not end there. For the main part the line is a sturdy English lower league player, honest and unassuming. But then there is the new signing, Continental and flash, full of flicks and tricks. I guess you have to choose which you prefer but, of course, there are parts to admire in both.

Like the Victoria Line the new service was created in the 1950's but LT waited until 1972 when it was authorised as "The Fleet Line". Funding was relatively straightforward: the government would pay for 75% of the line with the GLC picking up the bill for the rest. The plan was to relieve congestion on the Bakerloo. In the North East of the Bakerloo several branches ran into one causing delays, irritation, and inefficiency. The simple solution here was to exclude the branch line to Stanmore and have it taken over by the (now renamed) Jubilee, with a tunnel then dug from Baker Street to go all the way down to Charing Cross.

So that was the first and easiest part of the assignment, and that opened in 1979 with the inherited line from Baker Street to Stanmore and the new tunnel. The second ritzy part opened twenty years later- a time of market forces, sponsorship and marketing. The Northern part was cosy and even with the introduction of themed tiles on the stations (like the ones at Baker Street all Sherlock

Holmesy) there is no disguising the 30's feel and comfortable period charm. It's a genuine honest third division player. That could not be further from the eye or mind when wandering through the Blade Runner /S and M chambers of the Jubilee's finest new stations all definitely in the top flight.

Dark and brooding, with architectural awards by the score these stations are big, with large-scale staircases, oversize lift carriages, low lighting, exciting entrance halls. The Westminster Station journey is a really dramatic event, the lines are glass clad with inner doors on the platforms, sounds are muffled, there are TV monitors hanging everywhere, architectural light fittings, chains, unexplained shelving and alcoves in the semi darkness. You expect to see Kevin McCloud lurking behind every corner as it is a grand design.

The new stations and trains tie in perfectly with the perceived modernity of Docklands, the Olympics and all that entails. It serves a new and expanding East London population and it offers the journey in style. Canary Wharf's population has expanded from 15,000 to 90,000 in ten years, and most commute.

With the renovation of the Docklands area, the existing rail service (the DLR) seemed overloaded, the Jubilee extension branches off from the original line at Green Park and runs in tube a little way south of the Thames eastwards to the Docklands area, but continuing straight ahead when the river loops around the Isle of Dogs. The tubes then turn northwards and emerge north of the river, having crossed it three times in three stations. Finally, from Canning Town to Stratford a new surface line was built to one side of the existing NLR route. Now that the extension is open, the original line from Green Park to Charing Cross has been abandoned.

The costs were enormous, as grand as the scale of the stations. To begin with the budget was set at a £1.5 billion, but by the time the line ferried Tony Blair's guests to the Millennium Dome (now the O2) to party like it was 1999 because it actually was 1999, the costs had soared to £3.5billion. The added costs of meeting that deadline added millions.

How all that drama compares with the

other end of the line! Stratford is huge, impersonal, dwarfing the individual but providing an "enhanced customer experience" especially as you have to wander through the Westfields shopping centre to get to the street or the Olympics, whereas at the other end Stanmore is homespun, a local notice board has adverts for the Bowls Club or the bird watching society.

Now the Jubilee is the third busiest on the network and carries 213 million passengers a year, it has 27 stations, 13 below ground, and just 23 miles of track. The extension, with Premiership panache, was the first to use those sliding glass doors (platform edge doors) preventing both the double worries of draughts and suicides, there is step free access to the platforms and sound absorbent panels on the wall instead of tiles. It's a line of two halves but then London is too, and both the modernity of the capital and the history of this city are wrapped up in one line.

BELOW Millennium Dome (The O2 Arena) in Greenwich, London

Chapter 20

In Numbers

1 in 300 million The chance of any given tube journey resulting in a fatal accident.

2d The original flat rate fare of the Central London Railway, now the Central line, earning it the nickname "the Tuppeny Tube".

1.171billion Passenger journeys in 2012.

9.5% Percentage of customers travelling on open-boarding routes without valid tickets.

50m Tube journeys made annually using a Freedom Pass.

60 metres The length of the tube's longest escalator, at Angel.

270 Number of stations on the London underground.

59 The number of stations that arelisted buildings.

6.3km The longest distance between two adjacent stations, from Chesham to Chalfont & Latimer.

300m The shortest distance between two adjacent stations, from Leicester Square to Covent Garden.

265 The number of deaths on the tube in the past 10 years (excluding deaths from natural causes and terrorist attacks).

320 Number of steps on the longest

journey from surface level to platform, at Hampstead station.

BIGGEST, LONGEST

Each year, every Tube train travels **114,500miles/184,269km**.

The average speed of a train is **33km/20.5 miles per hour**.

Only **45 per cent** of the network is actually in tunnels.

There are **426** escalators. Waterloo has the most: **23**. The first was Earl's Court.

The total number of lifts, including four stair lifts, on the Underground network is **164**.

The deepest lift shaft is at Hampstead station and is **55.2m**.

The shortest lift shaft is at King's Cross and is just **2.3m**.

The total number of carriages in the Underground's fleet is **4,134**.

The total number of staff on the

Underground is approximately **19,000**.

Baker Street is the station with the most platforms: **10**.

The total length of the Tube network is **402km/249 miles**.

The longest continuous tunnel runs between East Finchley and Morden (via Bank) and is **27.8km/17.25 miles** long.

BELOW Hampstead station signage

Hampstead station

This spiral staircase has over 320 steps

Hampstead is the deepest station on the Underground and climbing this staircase is equivalent to a climbing a 15 storey building.

The longest distance between two stations is between Chesham and Chalfont and Latimer on the Metropolitan line, which are **6.3km** apart.

The shortest distance between two stations is from Leicester Square to Covent Garden on the Piccadilly line, which are a mere **300m** apart.

The longest journey you can take without a change is **59.4km** from West Ruislip to Epping on the Central line.

The longest escalator on the network is at Angel and is **60m** long, with a vertical rise of **26.5m**.

The shortest escalator is at Stratford, taking passengers up just **4.1m**.

The deepest station below street level in central London (not the whole system) is Bank, which is **41.4m** deep.

The first-ever day of public service was enjoyed by **40,000** passengers.

In 1908, the first full year of operation for all three lines, the Hampstead Tube (now part of the Northern Line) carried **25 million** passengers, the Bakerloo **28 million** and the Piccadilly **34.5 million**.

Passenger numbers grew rapidly and by 1918 the Underground was carrying **70 per cent** more people than in 1914.

Currently **1,107 million** passengers are carried every year.

82 million passengers travel through Waterloo each year.

SPEED AND DISTANCE

In central London, trains cannot drive faster than **30-40mph** because of the short distances between stations. **33km per hour** is the average speed of a tube train, including stops.

The Metropolitan line has the fastest train speeds, sometimes reaching over **60mph**.

Most distant places served to the North is Epping from Liverpool Street that's **27km** (**16 miles**). To the South Moorgate to Morden is **16km** (**10 miles**) and to the East Tower Hill to Upminster is **25km** (**15miles**) but furthest out is Aldgate to Chesham which

The longest journey possible without a change is on the Central Line West Ruislip to Epping, that's **54.9 km** or **34.1 miles**.

45% of the system is below ground of which 20 miles is in cut and cover and 93 miles in deep level Tubes.

INDIVIDUAL LINES

The Bakerloo runs from Elephant & Castle to Harrow & Wealdstone - **23km (14.5 miles)** - serves **25** stations

The Central runs from Ealing Broadway or West Ruislip to Woodford (via Hainault) or Epping - **74km (46 miles)** - serves **49** stations

The Circle runs from: Connects to most of London's National Rail termini - **27km (17 miles)** - serves **36** stations

The Hammersmith and City runs from Hammersmith to Barking - **25.5km (16 miles)** - serves **29** stations

The District runs from Upminster and Ealing Broadway to Richmond or Wimbledon, with other branches to Edgware Road and Olympia - **64km (40 miles)** - serves **60** stations

The Jubilee runs from Stanmore to Stratford - **36km (22.5 miles)** - serves **27** stations

The Metropolitan runs from Aldgate to Amersham, with branches to Chesham, Watford and Uxbridge - **67km (41.5 miles)** - serves **34** stations

The Northern runs from Morden to Edgware, Mill Hill East or High Barnet, with two central London branches - **58km (36 miles)** - serves **50** stations

The Piccadilly runs from Cockfosters to Heathrow or Uxbridge - **71km (44.3 miles)** - serves **53** stations

The Victoria runs from Walthamstow Central to Brixton - **21km (13.3 miles)** - serves **16** stations

The Waterloo and City runs from Waterloo to Bank - **2.4km (1.5 miles)** – there are no intermediate stations on the Drain.

Chapter 21

Odd Ditties
& strange facts

The Tube has become a part of popular culture, it is referenced in hundreds of songs, TV shows, films, pictures and plays, and as such it seems totally natural as it plays such a large part in people's lives The Underground should become an object of swirling mythology, misinformation and some great stories. There is also a huge amount of trivia from the Underground sometimes defying description and categorising in any other chapter!

TUBE BABIES

The most recent of many babies born on the underground was a boy, born in May 2009 on the Jubilee line-fortunately the mother had time to make it to a staff room helped by TfL crewmembers at London Bridge. But there have been a number of births, especially during the war, actually on the platforms. Perhaps the most celebrated is that of chat show host Jerry Springer and the US talk show veteran is probably the most famous person to have come into the world in a London underground station. He was born at Highgate station on 13 February 1944, where his mother had taken shelter from a Luftwaffe bombing raid.

But the first birth is still the oddest in that on May 13 1924 a baby girl was born actually on a Bakerloo train. Lord Ashfield was delighted and told the press she had been christened Thelma Ursula Beatrice Eleanor, thus gaining the initials TUBE. Unfortunately in the end it turned out not to be entirely true as she was named Mary Ashfield Eleanor, but good try.

COMMUNICATIONS

The Underground communicated with its' passengers to begin with in two ways, either through signage or by shouting at them. The guards and ticket collectors were frequently in good voice, and were known for their wit (at times) and for even their singing on occasion but as with most of the innovations it was Yerkes who instigated far more uniformity of signage, and then Lord Ashfield and specifically Frank Pick who got the whole system talking to their clients.

Pick hired a flow of consistently talented and creative artists to create some of the best poster art Britain has produced. Meanwhile in 1938 the shouting could give way to announcements with 120 stations having loudspeakers installed. A crackly disc was produced to encourage passengers to stand on the right, avoid impeding other travelers and keep moving on the escalators. In the 1970's the Victoria line and its' one-man trains

ABOVE A loudspeaker unit in use on a London Underground platform, 1941

meant that the driver could speak to the carriages.

Gradually the communication increased, now pre recorded messages tell us which station is next and when we are approaching it, both in rolling script on LED's and through the speakers, but you still occasionally get the charmingly diffident driver telling us from time to time, like a shy 17 year old guitarist at the microphone, "this ones for Dollis Hill, sit back...enjoy." Which leads us nicely to the most famous announcement of them all.

MIND THE GAP

Recently the newspapers carried the story that "the 40 year-old recording of the 'mind the gap' message played on the London Underground will be used once more so the widow of the actor behind the warning can hear his voice."

Oswald Laurence was heard for years on the Northern Line and lastly at Embankment station - where Dr Margaret McCollum would go just to hear her husband's voice after his death. Transport for London stopped using the message and understandably Dr McCollum was deeply upset to lose that last bit of contact with her husband.

But now, having been "touched" by the widow's story, TfL is using it again.

The original recording of "Mind the gap" was made in 1968 featuring the voice of

sound recordist Peter Lodge after he felt the actor booked for the session just could not get it right. There does after all need to be a suitable combination of authority, threat and irony, which is well beyond the powers of a number of actors who leap to mind.

While most lines still use Peter Lodge's recording of "Mind the gap", others use a recording by voice artist Emma Clarke. The Piccadilly line uses the voice of Tim

Bentinck, better known as David Archer from The Archers. Although used for a number of safety messages and played literally thousands of times Mr. Bentinck's fee was just £200, which is exactly £200 more than Peter Lodge's fee.

JUMPERS

The space below tube tracks are colloquially known as "suicide pits" as they help reduce the chance of death or serious injury should someone jump in front of a train. My wife experienced one at first hand, when on travelling home from work one hot sunny day before we met, she left the crowded carriage at Whitechapel feeling extremely woozy, walked straight across the platform and proceeded to fall in front of an incoming train. Luckily she landed, unharmed, in the pit. The train passed her, and fellow passengers pulled her semi conscious back to the platform. The first voice she then remembers is the station manager asking her if she had a valid ticket.

Around 50 passengers a year commit suicide on the Underground, however the Jubilee line is the only line to feature protective screens along the platforms.

METROLAND NO MORE

Although Metroland was built by the railways, Parliament prohibited other lines from profiting from the huge property price increases the advent of the Underground system brought to an area. Frank Pick argued that the Underground should be able to use the land they purchased as part of the building of the lines to develop, but he was told they had to sell it to property companies at cost thus

BELOW Map of "Metro-Land" and extension lines, published by the Metropolitan Railway in 1924

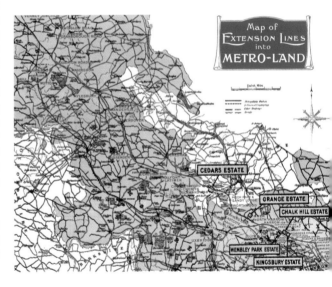

losing the five or six hundred percent profit the Underground had given to the area. It is ironic in a way insofar as the early investors in the Rail companies themselves tended to be construction companies who would benefit from the work generated.

THE STOP THAT NEVER STARTED

Passengers riding the Northern Line between Hampstead and Golders Green may have spotted the widened tunnels of North End station. In 1903, believing the area would be developed into houses for new commuters, Charles Yerkes's company, Hampstead Tube, began work on North End station beneath open farmland northwest of Hampstead Heath, they even created two platforms and planned to build more housing around it. But their plans met fierce local opposition, and in 1904 social reformer Henrietta Barnet actually purchased the farmland and protected it so it became known as the Hampstead Heath Extension. As a result in 1906, a year before the line was due to open, the company abandoned work on its half-built station. Henrietta then was

instrumental in setting up Hampstead Garden Suburb further north, but no Tube was added

The stop that never was kept going, however, and during the second world war a revived North End served as an underground bunker for Churchill's war cabinet. By the time of the cold war, the station had become part of the underground's flood defence system, accessed through an entrance hut disguised as an electricity substation. Then as secret as it could be, now publicly acknowledged North End functions as a storehouse for engineers and as one of the tube's many emergency evacuation routes.

FILMS AND MUSIC

2012 was a big year for the Underground. It featured as one of the star turns during the London Olympics ferrying literally millions of spectators to probably the most successful of modern day Games. It also got to star in a James Bond film, although the abiding memory of that role is of a train smashing through an underground chamber and ending up in a complete heap where Daniel Craig should have been standing. Fortunately the train was empty at the time.

But the Underground has been the star of popular culture, TV, books and the big screen more or less from the start. It's a superb place for action and chases (both The Bourne Ultimatum and Patriot Games did this before Skyfall). It's also a hidden world, things can be concealed, there are strange creatures down there, and the filming can be as consistent as working in a studio-you are in control of the lighting and there is no weather so film makers (as long as they work off hours and can meet the sky high location fees) are in their element.

I was once introduced to John Landis, and I complemented him on making the London traffic come to a stand-still at Piccadilly during his American Werewolf in London movie, I asked him if he planned to make any more like that and he replied laconically "Aw no the creature got away down the Tubes". Be warned.

Disused stations, known as "ghost" stations, such as those at Aldwych, Down Street and Lord's, often find alternative work as film and TV sets and the home

for 28 Days Later, Sliding Doors or even Prodigy music videos. Those naughty little fire starters were playing around near Aldwych.

In fact music has always had an affinity with the Tube. From Richmond (Ronnie Lane/The Faces) across to Muswell Hill or Waterloo (Ray Davies/The Kinks), no matter Who Are You (The Who) via a number of Suede tunes such as Saturday Night (the video for which was shot at Holborn Brett Anderson obviously travels a lot by Tube,) to Warwick Avenue (Duffy), or even Baker Street (Gerry Rafferty) Going Underground (the Jam) is something that happens again and again, Terry Disley for example has a sample of Mind the Gap on London Underground, a cool dinner jazz track. There is at least one massive Spotify playlist worth looking up and playing when you are commuting which is just full of great Tube related tracks you'll find it in search, very little Monochrome Set though surprisingly. For ukulele fans George Formby actually played during the war to shelterers. It made the sounds of the Blitz seem so much less scary.

There is always some live music down the Tube now. Since 2003, musicians require a license to busk on the Underground but now once on the list of accredited artists they have their own designated spaces, which is great because musicians playing in the carriages is always fairly embarrassing for everyone.

ART

The Underground has always been associated with modernity, and Pick used top British artists to push this idea further. Of course the Map itself is an artistic statement as well as a functioning tool,

at http://www.projectmapping.co.uk/Reviews/londonunderground you can find many different versions of the Map, adapted by artists, music fans or comedians to suit their ends. It is also worth knowing that the best selling poster in the UK relating to the Underground is the 1986 advert for the Tate Gallery by Tube by painter David Booth, with the lines all emanating from a tube of paint- it's a classic.

I have mentioned Henry Moore's sketches from the shelters, but work by Abram Games, Dora M. Batty, Eric Ravilious and R B Kitaj have been stuck on the walls over the years and literally hundreds of others including novelist Len Deighton. The range of work is so enormous it is bound to be variable, but some are brave, exciting and new-it is a treat for Londoners to have that in front of them everyday.

During the 150th anniversary travelers were treated with a major installation: Labyrinth by Mark Wallinger and 15 new works for 150, and TfL is keen on continuing Frank Pick's work with a whole series of innovative and reactive work, posters collections, film instal-lations. It's actually really good and all power to them for this.

In addition to the posters Scottish sculptor Eduardo Paolozzi designed the mosaic murals at Tottenham Court Road station, which were completed in 1984. Others have tried to join in but in the 90s, due to the boom in graffiti, the "silver" tube trains were replaced with the red, white and blue painted ones still seen today. The ceramics on the City and South London Railway (now part of the Northern line) were inspired by the designs of artist William Morris.

Southwark Station's blue cone wall, built as part of the Jubilee line extension's new generation of stations, was inspired by an 1816 stage set for The Magic Flute.

THE TUBE AS WORKSHOP

During the Second World War work had to stop on the expansion of the system. The extension to the Central line to Leytonstone, Hainault and Epping had been almost finished but the rails were yet to be laid when the war halted things. So the tunnels were used as long workshops to assemble components for

BELOW William Terriss, 1880

guns, tanks and aircraft with a small gauge railway put in to carry tools and components along the production line.

BECOMING VERSE

There has regularly been poetry on the Underground since 1986. Poets, some from the past, others still working have their lines reproduced on sta-

tion and tube walls amongst the adverts and posters. The idea was poet Judith Chermaik's idea. One of the first to be featured was Wordsworth's Composed Upon Westminster Bridge. There have been ten anthologies of "Poems on the Underground" published so far. I wonder if they thought of calling the book Tube Lines.

GHOST TRAIN

Over the years there have been many stories of hauntings on the Underground, and of course there are plenty of spooky works of fiction as well. The most famous ghost story is that of poor Anne Naylor who was murdered on the site of Farringdon station in 1758. Her screams are said to be heard every time the last train leaves the station. Meanwhile actor William Terriss is said to be staggering around Covent Garden over a century after he was stabbed there in 1897. The last reported sighting of William was in the 1970's. Obviously very reluctant to leave the stage.

There have also been many examples of drivers parking their tubes up for the night feeling they are being watched by a hidden pair of eyes, doors are left mysteriously open on carriages, and whispers can be heard on empty platforms. Let's face it an empty station is a scary place anyway and the ghosts of the many workers killed actually constructing the network are said to walk the lines at night.

The British Museum station, which is now closed, was reputed to be haunted by the daughter of Amen Ra, an Egyptian Pharaoh. She would appear and scream so loudly that the noise would carry down the tunnels as far as the adjoining Holborn station.

ABANDONED STATIONS

There are a number of abandoned stations in addition to British Museum, for example St Mary's Preston Road, Lord's, King William Street, to name but a few - it is quite a long list. They are the so-called Ghost Stations of London. There are also some that have lost platforms or been modernized leaving relics of a bygone era behind, a ventilation shaft where there is no need, a disused ticket hall, or an abandoned platform. The best resource I have found for this is the excellently comprehensive site of http://www. abandonedstations.org.uk/ which also has some terrific revelatory pictures on it.

The French site: http://carto.metro. free.fr/cartes/metro-london/ has a geographically correct underground map of London on it with some of the unused stations shown, it is really odd seeing the stations scattered out of their Beck context. For all things underground you can do a lot worse than visit the cheerfully subterranean site: http://www.subbrit. org.uk/

Of course the loss of a station often brought with it some inventive urban myth. South Kentish town opened in 1907 and closed 17 years later, it was just too close to other stations but the story goes that a careless passenger got off some years later when a train stopped at a signal, and then found himself abandoned on the "ghost" platform. Apparently it took him a week to attract the attention of the passing trains by lighting a fire amongst rubbish, and was rescued. Incidentally you can still see the remains of the ticket hall at street level and until fairly recently it was the home of an exotic looking (from the outside anyway, no info on the inside) massage parlour.

Chapter 22

The Map

The Underground map of London forms our mental picture of the city. It is the one essential accessory that every tourist coming to London needs, and it is blindingly simple, elegant and so clever all at the same time- when it was created it was a piece of cartography like no other in the world, both functional and unapologetically modern.

It was not always so with attempts to chart the Underground. Early attempts had the individual rail lines drawn over existing maps of London, so there was a confusion of routes, roads and places. It was especially confusing as those early lines did all follow existing roads.

It was Frank Pick who insisted on the use of the word Underground everywhere and in 1911 under Pick's instructions a map had been developed that did not have the streets on it, and every tube line was allocated a colour-although not the ones we use today. But the 1911 map although geometric was still geographically based, it looked straggly and unclear, a tangle of string really- a plate of vermicelli. This style held sway for the next twenty years but then came the bolt of lightening.

That's an appropriate metaphor as well because it was an electrician who came up with the design-Harry Beck produced his first sketch in 1931 and it was the simple forerunner of his masterpiece, a design that bounced around the globe

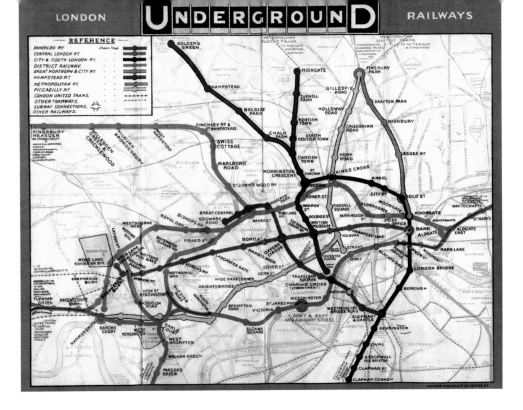

and set the level of the bar that has never been beaten. The sheer simplicity is what makes it special, Beck had worked as an electric draughtsman so used the connecting wires format, and an octagonal grid that just vanished for the ordinary viewer but it allowed him to make the lines meet at right angles. He did not care at all about the actual distance between stations on the map, so Great Portland Street for example looks a long way from Regents Park when they are less than 100 metres apart as the crow flies. Out in the suburbs the stations are a uniform distance apart even when in reality they were more than the rest of the line put

THE MAP

Keep up with the upgrade plan and how it might affect you at tfl.gov.uk

Transport for London 150 UNDERGROUND

Now I said Beck was an electrical draughtsman, well he was actually an unemployed electrical draughtsman having been made redundant by, that's right, the Underground Company. Once he submitted his historic design that would all change though, well not quite as they actually rejected the first version, but later they took him on part time and grudgingly accepted that maybe, just maybe, he was onto something.

Beck unwiggled the District and smoothed out the other lines, those heading out to the corners were given the same angles, and taking something from electronics he used a simple tick for the stations. He added the Johnston typeface and got it all to fit on a landscape format poster. He also exploited a really clever sleight of hand, or eye I should say, by enlarging the central section so the muddled middle could be seen and understood.

It was a stunning example of grace, style and a lack of clutter, a huge leap forward in branding as well giving the

ABOVE
Commemorative logo for the 150 anniversary of the London Underground Railway shown on the iconic Tube system map at Baker Street station

together. Beck's map is all about how to navigate the system and 80 years later it is still unbeatable and iconic.

The only topographical detail that is included, that truly shows the scale of London as a great City, is the River Thames with its cool blue course-again geometrically simplified-wending its way through the elegant and organised wiring diagram of the lines.

Underground when allied to the roundel and bar a thorough bit of corporate identity. The map became a symbol of London itself that no other system in the world can lay claim to. When you look at other subway system's maps there is none to touch it-some are charming like Valencia's simple lay out, Stuggart has a bizarre attraction, Nagoya a strange impenetrable lay out, the New York clutter is almost unreadable but represents a giant system, but even the Paris map looked better when given the Beck treatment at the start of the century.

That second version of the Beck London map had 750,000 pocket copies made of it and they all went in months. A poster was then produced and they were massively popular. They paid Beck for his work- he got 5 guineas (£5.25) for the map and £10 for the poster-and that was that. The equivalent of about £400 today for the best bit of graphic design we know of. Beck was an obsessive, he used to have a large version of the map laid out on his carpet in the drawing room at home in Finchley with additions sketched in, and he even used to sleep with a sketchbook under his pillow in case inspiration came in the middle of the night.

His relationship with LT was not smooth, he was never really honoured by them, as he should have been, a corporate middle manager played around with his design and even claimed the right to have his name on it not Becks. But reason prevailed and eventually Beck got a blue plaque and a whole section devoted to him in the London Transport museum. There was no point in carping anyway; he had got his £15 what was there to moan about.

The design by the way has made more profit for LT than any of the lines and the side business of taking passengers. They sell the map now on mugs, T-shirts, you name it and there are literally hundreds of versions of it - film star maps, music maps, animal maps, the list is endless-but then it is iconic.

A Blue plaque was unveiled on March 2013 at 14 Wesley Road, Leyton where Harry Beck was born in 1902, earlier in 2003 an 'unofficial' blue plaque for Beck had been placed by the Finchley Society at 60 Court House Gardens, West Finchley where Beck lived most of is life. He died in 1974.

LITTLE BOOK OF THE LONDON UNDERGROUND   139

Chapter 23

The Future

Eventually, the tunneling will stop but right now looking across the London landscape there seems to be as much activity from men with yellow hard hats on as there has ever been. Those massive ten million pound boring machines with names like Ada are right now hacking out the hole where Crossrail will go, in all some 26 miles of tunneling is tearing its way across town. Sometime they will stop and it will be in place and then the benefits of cross-town high-speed travel will be in place, but quite who these people are going to be who want to cross town regularly is yet to be divulged. The obvious benefits and the unstoppable social forces that created the Underground and shaped London which in turn created more change are now not quite so obvious.

It has to be said that it is also hard to imagine many new stations and any new lines within the confines of the current map, any expansion looks like being in the hinterland that London commands, but even then there is little logic with the existing railway network doing the job. With the still obvious exception of the South of London, the capital is well served. The way looks clear for those flying cars we were all promised in editions of the Eagle back in the 60s.

Beyond the spectacular Crossrail lies what has come to be known as Crossrail 2, a line that would link Hackney and

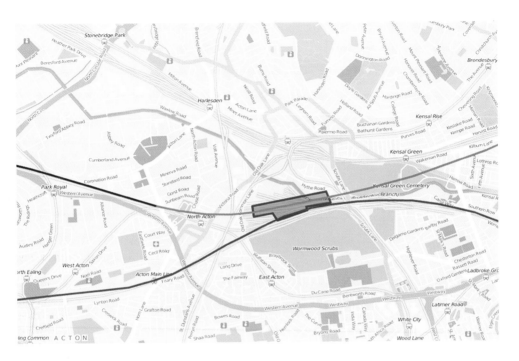

Chelsea with Kings Cross and Euston and Tottenham Court Road. There is an even more distant possibility, a so-called Crossrail 3 connecting Waterloo and Euston and therefore the main line rail services to and from the capital's north and south, and so far that has had provisional political support.

Otherwise, we're mostly looking at add-ons: the Northern Line extension from Kennington to Nine Elms and Battersea; a Metropolitan re-jig and a good look at the advantages of fully splitting the Northern Line at Camden Town station which would allow a large increase in capacity.

ABOVE Proposed Crossrail interchange from High Speed 2

tunnels faster thanks to better automated signaling systems. The trains will be automatic too of course. And maybe they will concentrate more on the suburbs. It is an odd statistic but most people who work in Canary Wharf actually commute from Surbiton so why not have more offices in Surbiton, or Finchley. Whatever changes the work pattern will change the Underground accordingly.

But for now the foreseeable future means that with Crossrail building stations fit for the next 100 years, places like Tottenham Court Road are going to be huge-six times the current size and I suspect as impersonal as some of the most capacious airline terminals.

But these little fiddles and Crossrail apart rather than some brilliant stroke, I suspect we are living with 'the upgrades" that seem to be going on pretty much interminably. With the system generally accepted to be at "capacity" the immediate solution seems to be longer stations, more standing room and longer trains whizzing through the

But as the Tube changes, whatever transformations are made the essential character of the Underground will

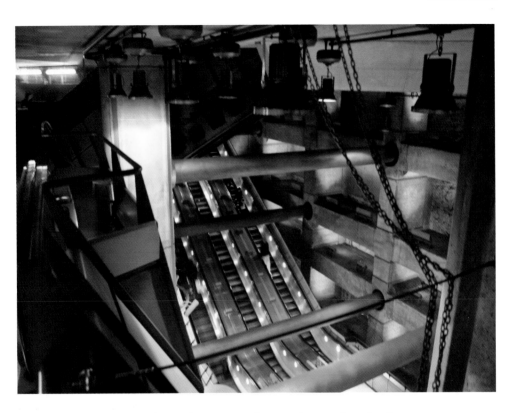

remain, the ties between the service and its' users are now too strong. Two World Wars, a consistent and ever replenishing stream of additions to Tube mythology and popular culture makes sure that somehow London always gets the system it deserves and needs. Meanwhile Londoners, despite the weekly grind of commuting, continue to enjoy going underground.

The pictures in this book were provided courtesy of the following:

WIKIMEDIA COMMONS & ROBIN BEXTOR

Design & Artwork: ALEX YOUNG

Published by: DEMAND MEDIA LIMITED & G2 ENTERTAINMENT LIMITED

Publishers: JASON FENWICK & JULES GAMMOND

Written by: ROBIN BEXTOR